Difficult People

Foolproof Methods- Dealing with Difficult People, Mean People and Workplace Bullying

William Lockhart

© Copyright 2015 - All rights reserved.

In no way is it legal to reproduce, duplicate, or transmit any part of this document in either electronic means or in printed format. Recording of this publication is strictly prohibited and any storage of this document is not allowed unless with written permission from the publisher. All rights reserved.

The information provided herein is stated to be truthful and consistent, in that any liability, in terms of inattention or otherwise, by any usage or abuse of any policies, processes, or directions contained within is the solitary and utter responsibility of the recipient reader. Under no circumstances will any legal responsibility or blame be held against the publisher for any reparation, damages, or monetary loss due to the information herein, either directly or indirectly.

Respective authors own all copyrights not held by the publisher.

Legal Notice:

This book is copyright protected. This is only for personal use. You cannot amend, distribute, sell, use, quote or paraphrase any part or the content within this book without the consent of the author or copyright owner. Legal action will be pursued if this is breached.

William Lockhart

Disclaimer Notice:

Please note the information contained within this document is for educational and entertainment purposes only. Every attempt has been made to provide accurate, up to date and reliable complete information. No warranties of any kind are expressed or implied. Readers acknowledge that the author is not engaging in the rendering of legal, financial, medical or professional advice.

By reading this document, the reader agrees that under no circumstances are we responsible for any losses, direct or indirect, which are incurred as a result of the use of information contained within this document, including, but not limited to, — errors, omissions, or inaccuracies.

Table of Contents

Introduction 9

Chapter 1: Difficult Behavior 17
    The angry ones 18
    The dominating ones 18
    The pessimist ones 18
    The stubborn ones 19
    The free riding ones 19
    The drama queen 20
    The under achiever 20
    The over achiever 20

Chapter 2: Types of Difficult People 29
    The Know-It-All 29
    If your boss is the egoist 33
    The colleague who knows it all 34
    If the egoist is working for you 35
    The Super Agreeable 41
    The Chronic Complainer 53
    Why is it not good to be a Chronic Complainer? 56
    Steps on how to deal with complaints: 61
    The Unresponsive Ones 64
    The Silent and Quiet ones 64

How to respond to the unresponsive ones effectively 65
The Indecisive, the Ditherer, the Hesitant 71
Dealing with a waffler coworker 71
How to communicate well with a waffler: 74
The Negative 77
Why is it not good to be a Negativist? 80
Dealing with the pessimists: 82
The Aggressive and Offensive 86
The Sherman Tank 87
How to deal with a Sherman Tank 88
The Sniper 91
Howto deal with a Sniper 92
The Exploder 94
How to deal with an Exploder 95

Chapter 3: How to Deal with Difficult People? 97
Reforming Steps 98
Survival Steps 100
How to define difficult 102
The boss who took credit for my work 104
The boss who didn't trust me enough to do things 106
A colleague who mocked that I was no longer young 107
Colleagues that ganged up together and made fun of people 108
The Office Romeo 110

The physical abuser 111
Emotional abusers 112

Chapter 4: Bullying 115
How to Identify Symptoms of Bullying? 117
Knowing the difference between Harassment and Bullying
.... 120
Psychology behind Bullying 121
Workplace Bullying 123
Effects of Workplace Bullying 125

Chapter 5: Conflict 133
Interpersonal 135
Change related (Trends) 136
External Factors 136
Organizational 137

Chapter 6: Cooling Conflicts 139
Steps on how to deal with Conflicts 139
Your part in any given situation at work 145
Teams 146
People who waste time 149
The Qualities that Make a Person Likeable 151
Honesty 152
Integrity 153
Are you friendly and encouraging? 153

Patience 154
Willing 155
Exercises to Help Your Patience Levels 156
Practicing Mindfulness 158
Why People are Difficult in General 162

Conclusion 167

Introduction

People - basically, this book is all about people, their complexities and understanding them. Understanding people solely, (not including situations, timing, place and the likes) is a very broad concept in which professionals, doctors and mentors in particular find it challenging to completely predict and study how the human brain works with relation to a person's behavior and attitude. In simple terms, a person is a very dynamic individual that cannot be relied to having the same response to every details and situations he may have for the rest of his lifespan. How can a professional completely understand something if **he** is a factor in the study itself? The Creator is the only one who perfectly knows his creations, like an inventor knows its invention.

Science, however, can somehow explain different personality types humans possess. The possibility of the combination and variety of emotions, reactions, behavior, innate attitude and mental process a single person can have is too broad and complicated to fully understand and perfectly sum up in a book. However, most types that do upset others in the workplace do fall into categories quite nicely and we can deal with these, helping you to overcome difficulties with these people when you have to work with them.

Saying all these things, let me introduce you to what this book will be all about. Given all the complexities and wide range of human personalities, there will always be that kind of person whom you will label to as difficult.

What really does come to your mind when you hear the word difficult? As Merriam-Webster Dictionary defines it, Difficult means, *"requiring much work or skill to do or make"*, *"not easy to deal with or manage"*, *"not willing to help others by changing you behavior: stubborn or unreasonable"* or in full definition, *"hard to do, make, carry out, deal with, manage, overcome, or understand."*

With all these definitions being relevant, the common ground we see is that it always involves being hard to deal with. Let's relate it to people. We can therefore state that difficult people are those who need more effort to harmoniously deal with and take a lot more understanding than all others. Right now, you might be thinking of some people you know who might actually labeled as to being one of them. However, I want you to skip that part of your brain working and let's start with you. Yes you.

All people, including you and me, have some attitude within themselves that can be considered as difficult. Before we try to analyze and study anybody else, let us start with you. Questioning others may be more complicated than questioning yourselves and evaluating your own attitude. What can you say about yourself? Do you think your friends and colleagues label you as a difficult person? Let me tell you something. Good and nice people are not always the same as you. There are a lot of factors involved in determining whether a person is nice or difficult such as different culture, backgrounds and upbringing and it's not limited to these differences. We can never perfectly tell whether you'd be in the good or difficult range of people, because it depends from whose viewpoint you are looking. You can be exceptionally difficult if the person judging you finds that you do not respond in the way that they expected you to.

In this book we will focus specifically on dealing with these difficult people in the *workplace*. This is the place where not only your professional skills are required but also your professional behavior and attitude towards any situation that would be presented.

As we go along classifying and understanding the types of people and how to deal with them, I want you to remember this rule that you will be needing to bear in mind all throughout this book. DO NOT TAKE IT PERSONALLY. It really isn't personal. It's all about accepting your own shortcomings and remembering that others have their point of view as well.

As Albert Einstein once said, "You have to learn the rules of the game. And then you have to play better than anyone else."

You do not want this type of person to get in the way of your professional road to success do you? So we must always remember to set personal issues aside when dealing with them in the workplace. Moreover, keep in mind that you always want to get the most out of every situation you may encounter whether you're dealing with this type of individual or not. Always remember to ask yourself these important self-assessment questions: "What do I want to achieve in this particular encounter?" "How will I benefit from this?", "Do I need to change my behavior in order for me to reap a positive outcome?" And the list goes on.

The important thing is you do not lose track of your purpose as far as the first question pertains. Always remember that the only person you have the capacity to change is you. Your behavior is the only thing you can control in a certain situation and not the other person's attitude that you are dealing with. You must use this control to your full advantage. No matter what happens, at the end of the day, the shocking truth is that they don't care about you. Yes. No matter how paranoid you may be rethinking of a certain encounter, none of it will matter when you step outside of the office. And so always remember to know your purpose in any time or in any situation, keep your focus, maintain a professional relationship and succeed in achieving what you need without compromising your own values.

As we go along in this book, you will learn how to determine these types of people, categorize them, and know how to specifically deal with each type of person. One simple rule I want you to remember is that, difficult people are always predictable depending on how you classify them. For example: if you know someone who is a great complainer, would you be surprised if you come into the office and you hear him complain about the weather and stuff? I bet you wouldn't. Therefore, the simple key is to know what type of difficult people they are and know how to effectively deal with them in any given situation.

In our daily lives, we encounter a lot of people and each of them has a unique personality and behaves accordingly. Different types of personality may clash with each other, which can lead to difference in opinions and eventually end in arguments.

However, there are instances where we come across "difficult people", people who are really hard to manage and deal with.

Dealing with such people can often lead to aggression and frustration, which can affect our personal lives. Often we ourselves can be difficult in some situations but are not able to realize it. An extreme case of difficult behavior is "bullying" which is sadly becoming more and more common these days. With the rise in the number of suicides and other deaths due to bullying, it has no longer remained a personal problem.

It is now time to address and understand this difficult behavior as early as possible, before it gets worse. This book tries to understand the psychology behind the actions of difficult people and ways to cope up with them. It tells you about ways in which people with "mean traits" can be helped and also how not to let them affect our own behavior. We will also learn about bullying with a special focus on "workplace bullying."

As more and more people are stepping out of their homes to take their place in the work environment, there is an increase in the number of cases of workplace bullying. Often very hard to recognize, workplace bullying can slowly take on a very ugly form and affect a lot of lives.

I hope that you learn a thing or two about mean personalities and bullies and ways to confront them throughout this book. I want to thank you for choosing this book and I believe it will clear all your doubts regarding bullying from the perspective of both the culprit and the victim. Only by knowing both sides can you actually achieve what it is that you crave and start to enjoy your work environment much more than you do now.

Let's get started!

William Lockhart

Chapter 1
Difficult Behavior

First of all we need to understand the exact definition of difficult behavior. It is characterized by one or many of the following traits: gossiping, refusing to acknowledge others, being rude, harassing, complaining constantly, ignoring and being insensitive to others' needs etc. It may even include those with high expectations that lay those expectations on other people's doorsteps.

Difficult people may be too self-centered, too gloomy or too needy. We also need to understand that if a person is actually difficult or it's us who are at fault. We can easily brand others as problematic or mean, while in reality we might be doing things in a wrong way. Here are a few steps by which we can identify typical mean traits in people:

William Lockhart

The angry ones

These people will be constantly angry. They will regularly find ways to argue and create conflicts. Such people are often found quarrelling with their colleagues and might even resort to yelling and harming the other person physically. These are angry individuals. They may have problems with their personality, with their home life, but mostly they have problems with their attitude toward others.

The dominating ones

These people will always try to dominate others. They will readily express their opinions but will not like it if others do not share the same viewpoint. They get easily frustrated when they find people not following their ways or ideas. Often these are people who are not tolerant and who have little empathy. They don't have the patience to listen to excuses and would certainly not accept them. The dominant people are those that employees may be afraid of. They intimidate and make people feel useless, even when they are not.

The pessimist ones

These are the people who are never satisfied. No matter how hard people try to please them or how good the things are, they will always find ways to complain. They are continuously trying to find nooks in any situation and can bring down the energy level of any gathering quickly. If you think of the energy levels that you get out of life. The pessimist will always make everything seem worse and will indeed try to drag everyone down to his/her level because they have no way to control that pessimism.

The stubborn ones

These people have rigid ideas and it's very hard to convince them otherwise. They are not ready to change themselves even when they realize that it is for their own good. Often they land in troublesome situations but still won't listen to others. These are people who cling to the notion that they know better than others even if they don't. They may not listen to reason and may make mistakes and blame others.

The free riding ones

These people are often encountered at workplaces. They will always try to rob people of their credits. They can be very manipulative and know well how to turn tables in their direction. The free rider is the one who is the least stressed, who has the emptiest desk but who gives the impression that they work harder than anyone else in the office. They leech energy from others and use people.

The drama queen

These are people who have to have all of the attention, even if they don't merit it. Their dramas are usually mundane but they see them as being more important than anything else.

The doormat: Believe it or not, the doormat isn't making life easier for people within the workplace. They may think that they are, but they let other people walk all over them – usually because they have no sense of self-esteem and see this as the normal way for people to treat them. Why is this a problem? Because it makes room for the opportunist and means that equal balance within the workplace cannot be achieved.

The under achiever

These are people who are well qualified to do a job but who do the very minimum within the workplace because it is their nature to back away from responsibility. It's a shame because they have the intelligence to actually achieve, but don't seem to have the impetus to do that.

The over achiever

Just as the under achiever is a problem for others, the over achiever is as well. They set boundaries that are too high for others and thus make others look inefficient or even unworthy within the workplace situation. The over achiever isn't a winner because he/she doesn't have any empathy at all for others and will never work as part of a team unless they are leading it.

These traits might be present in combination with each other in a person. Most of them overlap each other in behavioral pattern. Also, a person is difficult when these traits are constantly observed in him or her. Sometimes, we all can behave in a problematic manner but that does not mean that we are difficult. It is human nature to err and there will be instances when we will show the above mentioned traits. It only becomes a problem when it is occurs continuously and deteriorates a person's relationship with others. Apart from these qualities, there might be an attribute or so that can make handling a person difficult. For instance, dealing with a person who is never on time and always takes others for granted can be very frustrating.

They are only difficult if the trait keeps re-occuring

Let's take a close look at each of these types because there may be reasons why they behave in the manner that they do. You need to have a better understanding of their reasoning because this is where empathy plays a role. Stepping into the shoes of another person may help you to understand them better. Remember, that even if a person displays bad behavior in the work place, you need also to examine your relationship with that person to see if you are seeing what everyone else does or whether you are biased by your own beliefs. That's important, because if you are affected by your own feelings, you may be able to make adjustments to the way that you perceive things to make life easier.

Angry people are usually angry for a reason. Perhaps there is something in their home life that is unsatisfactory. I once knew someone within this category and it turned out that he was a very sad case indeed. In his home life, he had a domineering woman. She would not let him do the things that he wanted to do and the result was inner turmoil and anger. The only place that he could let this surface was in the workplace. So how do deal with it? Sometimes, validating someone who is angry is enough. They are fighting for some kind of validation that they don't get elsewhere. It was obvious from the guy's attitude that he didn't like women very much because of his experience throughout life with women. Thus, the women in the office decided to show him another side to women – a nurturing side that wasn't going to allow his anger to make their lives miserable, but who cared enough to listen to the guy. You need to find out why someone is angry and that's not always easy to do. Sometimes, people are not even aware that they are angry.

Angry people also need to be watched carefully. How do they respond to your replies? How do they respond to others? Sometimes you need to compare this because they may be like this with everyone and perhaps others have a thicker skin and are able to dismiss the anger because they accept that the individual talks in that way. Look at the interaction with others and perhaps you may learn what it is that you do that makes them angry. Chances are it isn't personal. It's merely a question of knowing how to respond.

Pessimists are a little easier to deal with because these are people who see everything in a bleak manner. Often they depend upon people taking notice of them. If you find yourself with a pessimist, being cheerful around them and telling them that their negativity is actually bringing you down isn't that bad a thing to do. They may be so wrapped up in their own pessimism that they don't see the backlash or appreciate what it does to others when they are so negative. If you really cannot change them, change your own attitude toward them and ignore the pessimism. Tell yourself that they are doom mongers and distance yourself from their negativity. There is hope for the pessimist, as a scientific report from the BBC told how twins, one of whom was positive while the other was negative dabbled in mindfulness meditation to overcome negativity. If you think that your work colleague could be receptive to the idea, drop some literature onto their desk because it may change their outlook of the world in general. You could always invest in an eBook on mindfulness meditation and tell them you are reading it to encourage them to read it. It may change their way of looking at things for the better.

William Lockhart

There is not much that you can do about stubborn people. They are born that way and there's not much you can do to change them. However, stubborn people do have a negative side. If you know what tasks they are capable of doing and keep them away from tasks which may fail due to their stubborn attitude, you will find that they excel in those tasks making their stubbornness a positive value to the office or workplace rather than a detrimental one.

Free riders need to be handled as soon as you notice it happening. If everyone around you agrees that they are freeloaders, then they need to have this spelled out and be deprived of things that other people get through recognition of good work. They bring down others in the workplace because they like to take the credit for things. This kind of person needs to be taken down a peg or two to show them that there isn't any room for people who don't pull their weight.

As for the drama queen, there's an easy way to solve this from disrupting the office. If people are bringing personal grievances and miseries into the office, then it's time to step in and tell them that after hours is when stuff like that should be talked about. People like this are usually a little insecure, so be gentle, but let them know that their dramas are getting in the way of work and that it isn't fair on others within the working environment to have to listen to the dramas every day of the week. Some will respond in a sympathetic way, but when it comes to upsetting the balance of the whole workplace, they do need to be told to keep their personal life out of the office.

Over achievers and under achievers may need to be switched to jobs that allow them to want to achieve equally. Sometimes it is as simple as that. The over-achiever doesn't want to be part of a team, so needs to be placed in a job where teamwork isn't the main way of doing things, while the under-achiever needs nurturing and teaching. Perhaps using different teaching methods will work effectively.

Whatever type of person you find yourself working with, you need to remember that you have a type too. You may be intolerant. You may be difficult to work with because of this. Look at yourself and work out why there is so much negativity at work. I once did this and what I found shocked me. What I found was that I was the reason people were negative. I had laid out expectations that some could not meet. What I had actually produced was an environment where over-achievers ruled and where under-achievers struggled to keep up with others and was extremely unhappy and negative. They even made up dramas to cover up their inadequacies, but I hadn't been a good person for them to work with because not only had I not noticed that they were struggling to keep up. I hadn't done anything to address it.

When I worked out what was wrong, I used the stronger members of staff to help the weaker members and split the group into teams, so that each team had a strong leader and I instructed them to come up with creative ways to explain the parts of the job that the slower members were having difficulty with. We paid on results, but what was the most fascinating thing to watch was how creative people adjusted their teaching methods to achieve a good result. Once you understand that everyone's learning capacity is not the same – you can use different methods, which the slower members of staff are more comfortable with to get them over the hurdle of learning. As soon as this happened and they understood better what was expected of them, there was vibrancy within the office that spelled real success and people – including me – were happier.

Sometimes you not only have to look at the personalities. You also need to look at changes that can be made to suit the personalities better. When you do that, you create harmony even though these people come over as difficult. The difficulties may be the system of working or the system of explaining things. Learn to be empathetic. Learn to put yourself into other people's shoes and then you get to know what's wrong and can do something about

Difficult People

it. I once had an awful boss. We all despised him, but what we hadn't realized was that he was insecure. All of the other bosses in different offices had University degrees. He didn't and was in fact carrying around a worry that one day they may decide that his qualifications were not good enough to have that job. What he was doing to compensate was trying too hard and in doing so, alienating people around him. Once we knew what the problem was and showed him loyalty, he turned out to be the best boss I ever had.

William Lockhart

Chapter 2
Types of Difficult People

In this part of this book, you will be able to classify difficult people according to their specific point of attitude problem. This will serve as a quick guide for you to determine different persons in the workplace who you would be dealing with. However, these classic seven types do not completely include every single difficult person you may meet in the workplace. Simply these would be the general seven types you would typically meet. Are you ready to meet them?

The Know-It-All

Knowing and understanding the egoist

Have you ever met someone who talks like he's the only person in the world to know everything or is being such an egomaniac that he really makes you feel stupid just listening to all his blabbering?

William Lockhart

I bet we all do have that one person in mind that actually acts and communicates like this. Well, unfortunately, working with these types of people isn't so easy.

A Know-it-all, although he may not be aware that people are aware of who he is and what he wants, has an exceedingly huge amount of need to be praised and be recognized for his intellectual skills that he always boasts about. Know-it-alls are a bore, exceptionally dreary and are dull. They can provoke a feeling of anger towards the person they are with, cause resentment and in rare but important cases even resort to violence.

Some studies made in the late 90's have shown that know-it-alls may have some issues regarding the grave need of self-importance or even maybe being not able to contribute, participate and to be a part of a certain group's level of pool of thoughts and ideas in which he has a strong conviction deep inside that he could be worthy enough of participating. However, the studies concluded that listening to a know-all's unending speeches could result to impractical usage of time that could somehow be used in finishing certain more important tasks.

Know-it-alls can be very complicated at times. They can have many characteristics and even overlap other difficult types. Some may even be considered as bullies that we will discuss in the latter part of this book. They will be very consistent with their words and insist that they are right and it will seem to you that there is not much point in trying to make them see otherwise. They are extremely compelling or convincing in their approach. As I have pointed out in the first part of this chapter, they act like they are talking to a child who doesn't have any idea of what he is saying and that definitely is very annoying. The know-it-all knows it all and that's the problem. People don't actually know it all.

Whenever in a group meeting, the know-it-all often stands out in speaking what he thinks he actually knows with the idea that nobody in the room could actually have that in mind or could contradict what he was saying. They seek attention from everyone, making everyone feel stupid but in reality they are the ones who look silly. They like being the center of attention, and will always try to govern every conversation. One problem is if they read something legitimate like the news or somehow they will feel like an expert about that particular topic without even considering the fact that they have a very limited knowledge about it because it only came from one source and obviously do not completely understand every detail. Moreover it is not important for them to make up facts or pretend to know everything even if it's a lie.

William Lockhart

Some people say that these kinds of people are hard to deal with, especially in the office. The truth is they're not. The trick is for you to remember that at the end of the day you'd still get to work with these people and you should keep your cool and still act professionally. Remind yourself of what you really want.

The Dalai Lama once said that: "Whenever you talk you are just repeating what you already know, but when you listen you might learn something new." - A thought worth bearing in mind is that all know-it-alls have a problem dealing with since they don't listen. They tend to be referred to as the egoists, the self-centered, the insecure, the show-offs, the attention seekers and the ones who are easily flattered. So why do people find it difficult to work with such people?

Good communication is a basic necessity that every organization's group should have. It doesn't matter what the age of the group you belong to in the office or the number of years you spent there. Being a know-it-all indicates a bad attitude that could result in negative feedback from other people in the workplace. Remember that work is all about being part of something and egoists who think that they know it all don't actually feel that they are a part of something. They are the something! This is dealt with sometimes by simply agreeing to differ and sometimes by educating the know-it-all so that what he knows is really valid.

Since he won't listen without some kind of validation, it's a tricky balancing act but you can do it. "Do you remember that idea that you had about reshuffling the staff?" validates his idea. Then you can expand upon it and make him think that the idea was his. That works well with a know-it-all because they feel they are getting the credit for something, regardless of whether it was their idea or not.

If your boss is the egoist

Flattery. That's the easiest tactic you could ever use for every single egoist. Remember that you don't have to take the credit for every idea you have to pass every single time. Give him the credit once in a while. Flatter him as if he's the one who did the great job. After all, it is like saying you have a wider thinking than him. You focus on executing the job well and not on taking the praise of the others while your ego maniac boss enjoys the praise. Do you have any idea in mind that you want to get past your egoist boss? You can try this as it sometimes works well to your advantage:

"I've read the email you sent out about redesigning our old plan in our eastern division. You know, I think you have a great, creative and unique idea. Taking this into consideration, I think we might want to add a few things."

Do you think your boss will have any interest in your ideas and take a little time to read and think about your idea? Yes he will. Egoists are blind. They only see themselves. Even if you couple him with a few co-workers or even in a group with all of his staff, he will only listen to himself. Does this sound like a big trouble to you? Yes if you are too sensitive and you're not confident in doing your own job. However, if you are truly good at what you do, your co-workers will eventually know whose ideas it was coming from, so do not worry about taking the credit. Instead keep on being excellent in doing your work and keep on keeping that egoist boss in the loop by acknowledging his part in everything that you do.

The colleague who knows it all

When dealing with a colleague who just can't stop boasting at you all the time, always remember to stick to the facts and do not prick their bubble. Let them know that you are particularly interested in the actual facts that they are saying and not the side where they are making themselves too important. Stick to the facts and figures that you would need to initiate the work you are assigned to in order for you not to become biased on anything. Asking a question like, "Well that's good. Just what greater percentage on sales did you really achieve this quarter as opposed to last month?" No matter what response you get from them, you have made it clear that you are just interested in facts they can provide.

Soon the bragging will stop if you show them how uninterested you are to those unimportant things they keep on saying. The trouble with someone who brags is that if it doesn't work, there's little point to doing it. They will go off and brag to someone else and thus your life will be made easier.

If the egoist is working for you

Being a leader of a team is a very challenging role especially in terms of motivating them to work together for a single purpose that would include teamwork and discipline. You may not want an egomaniac getting in the way grabbing all the credit and not be able to achieve a sole success created and worked duly by the team. However, if you do have that kind of person in your team, you could still motivate him to your group's advantage. Try saying to him something like "I know and I've seen you've been being pretty good at your work. I would honestly appreciate it if you could try to help the team, as well in keeping up a high standard of performance so we all get our own fair share of credit and me. Would you be willing to help me with that?" The fact that you have enlisted their help will give them the impetus they need to actually assist you.

Appeal to his ego. Get him to work for the team. He will be flattered and at the same time you would achieve your planned results. An egoist needs his ego stroked a little to get what you want out of them. If you tell him he is an egoist, he will go off in the opposite direction and will potentially get other team members to side with him that is not healthy for teamwork. There are always those who are easily fooled by their egotistical stories.

Additionally, here are 8 tips on how you can handle this egomaniac person:

1. Under all circumstances, avoid including your boss in the issue unless the egomaniac person is truly affecting the outcome of your work success.

   According to Isa Adney, author of "How to Get a Job without a Resume" and the blog firstjoboutofcollege.com,

   "If that becomes necessary, maintain a positive tone and instead of complaining about the person, focus on what you're willing to do to make sure the work is done well,"

   Always remember to act and speak professionally and do not let personal matters affect you in speaking up to your boss. The problem with going to the boss is that it makes you look weaker and incapable of dealing with your own problems and that's not going to be a good thing to have on your resume.

2. Focus on Constructive Criticism on their behavior instead of taking on the issue personally.

Remind yourself that maybe this person is all-out clueless about his bad behavior toward others. He may not be aware that his actions affect so many people and the work in the office. If that is the case as you may have observed, try talking to that person in a private manner and place somewhere away from the office. Try to point out his flaws in a gentle and more importantly in a respectful way so that he can view it as an improvement spot for himself.

A know-it-all may be a highly insecure person so remember to stroke their ego, flatter them wisely and only within their range of knowledge but also caution them on their behavior on how it affects the others especially those people who need a little more backup in terms of speaking up due to lack of confidence. Typical sentences that work would be "I know you have your own way of doing things, but we need to find a way that works for everyone." He may even help you to find that way and you may in turn be able to validate him by letting people know it was his idea.

3. Remember to scrutinize important details

    Do not be afraid to confront the person and further ask questions on where their expertise or authority is coming from. Asking know-it-all specific details will teach him to check his facts first before bragging and speaking up. If you need to know something factual, then don't be afraid to ask for it and to expect them to answer your questions. This may make them think twice about giving information that is erroneous.

4. Always pack up your sense of humor

When leaving the house and making your way to the office you may not want to keep a serious face all the way to the end of the day. A little fun may be the best way to cheer up your day and this may rub off on your co-workers too.

When it comes to the know-it-all, the last thing you want to do is to make them feel unimportant by not getting any attention at all. Keep in mind that you are maintaining work life balance in the workplace and keeping a know-it-all in the company takes a little more effort than the others.

If you are caught in a highly tempting conversation with him and you want to backfire with sarcasm, always remember that it will not lead to a very positive result. You must be aware that you have a wider understanding approach and must not step down to his level of attitude. Instead of creating a disagreement, why not try to laugh it off? Of course this should be in a friendly and respectful way. Create a harmonious and a very light environment for your particular situation.

5. Always arm yourself with true and complete facts

   Being prepared is a key to success. Never come to the office and face you bosses or your colleagues presenting an idea you are not confident and sure about. Always remember to verify all the information you gathered and double check your sources. The more you are armed with verified facts, the lesser the chance that you would be bombarded by questions from this know-it-all. Keep your information in writing so that when questions come up you will have something to share with the team. In any case it might be useful or needed. Never leave everything in your mind. Back up your knowledge in writing. It's always better to be safe than sorry.

6. Be a good role model

   In being a leader, say for example you're the manager or head of a team, there would be some cases in which it's okay to admit that you do not know things and you will be needing help from others. Acknowledging others' opinion indicates you are flexible and a good and active listener to your subordinates. At the same time you will somehow build trust and knit your team together closely because of your openness. Remember that a leader should not only be a great motivator and speaker but a good and attentive listener as well.

7. Choose your battles wisely

   It's not always the case that you should entertain a know-it-all. Sometimes a simple thank you as a respectful way of ignoring their way of helping can come in handy. Let's admit that dealing with a know-it-all can sometimes exhaust you to the point that you just want to be alone. You would not want to ruin your day just because a person like that wants to share something that would not in any way be beneficial to you. So, choose your battles wisely.

8. Show some empathy

   Always remember that no matter how this co-worker annoy or irritate you, whether he's doing it on purpose or just not aware of what he's doing, his know-it-all attitude might be a result of a personal issue somewhat deeper than you know. Instead of losing your temper and ruining your day, showing some empathy could be a better option for the both of you. Besides, at the end of the day, you would still be co-workers who should know how to deal with each other harmoniously. Try to step into his shoes and understand why he sees things in the way he does. Try to find the underlying problems and address them within the workplace. This will help in long term goals and in cementing relationships between workers.

The Super Agreeable

How to spot and deal with a Mr. Nice Guy

Please take note that being an agreeable type of person is not always a bad idea. What we will be discussing here are those types of people who take being an agreeable and nice person to the extent that it is no longer normal or acceptable and would perhaps be a factor in rising conflicts in the office. So what do we mean by saying they could create or initiate a conflict? Isn't a good thing that a person always agrees to everything delivered to him? Well let's take a deeper look into this super nice type of person.

The good sides:

Very attentive

The super agreeable person listens well to people who give their time talking to him. He enjoys being given attention as well and so makes it a habit to give back in return the same amount of attention and focus given to him. While the know-it-all doesn't enjoy listening attentively to others and focusing keenly on details, the super agreeable enjoys being able to learn something from the other person or people. If you just want to talk and you do not mind what response you may get, whether it would be helpful or not, the super agreeable is the one to go to.

Always Smiling

Well it's not a basic or necessary description of the super agreeable but generally speaking, he can be very positive and share good vibes with you whenever he is around and spreads happiness among people. He tends to prioritize happiness throughout his day so no matter what happens he will just go with the flow and agree with everything that may be given to him. A smile indicates positive feedback to the super agreeable and since he likes to be around people, a smile is a great tool for him to be closer to the others he works with. Who doesn't like to be smiled at anyway?

Sociable

The super agreeable, putting it simply, loves to be around people. He gives importance to people whom also love hanging around with him. He doesn't find it very hard mingling with other people and communicates well on every topic a group is talking about. He could be referred to as a jack-of-all-trades when it comes to group or personal conversations. Whatever you say to him, whether it be within his interest or not, as long as you are focusing on him he will have a lot of things in mind to say. Here, the focus is on the other person the super agreeable is dealing with. He actually doesn't care too much for himself, but rather what the other person or the group's interest may be. In a way, he could be a little bit selfless on this part.

Outgoing

In relation to being a very sociable person, the super agreeable is pretty much very outgoing also. People with this kind of attitude can be sometimes classified as being an extrovert, warm, friendly, easy going, lively and affectionate person. There would be no problem when group parties or outings will be involved. It is very important for him not to be left out and always belong to the group. He should know everything that is going on and at the same time have something to add to it. They participate actively in all plans and tasks the group has even if they had no single idea on how to take action that may be considered appropriate. For him, what matters most is the talking. He wants to agree with everything so that he could belong and work harmoniously with the group.

Personal with others

Sometimes, these people pleasers tend to be very personal to others to gain the attention they want. Being personal with others do not generally impose a negative situation, however, it does need to have limitations, which these types of people have somewhat of a problem dealing with. Relationships are very important to them so they sometimes set aside other important factors such as being too personal to others.

Helpful and supportive

A super agreeable type of person is always on the go when a colleague or friend is in need. The focus here is to attend to their needs without the purpose of taking on extra work because of it. Sometimes, this person is not aware that he cannot actually do the job. Taking initiative in helping to finish the task doesn't really concern him at all. This type of co-worker may be a good type of partner for you to have when you look at it on the outside, but taking things closely, and if you really take time to look at his actions or performance, you might want to check your view upon his performance.

The bad sides

People-pleasers

In general, the super agreeable can be synonymous to people pleasers. It is a very precise, exact though broad definition of them. They value relationships with people so much that they have this vague distinction between the truth and lies. For them, as long as it will please the other person or the group they would simply agree to it without first checking the facts. In the workplace, relationships with your co-workers are very important, however, being a people-pleaser doesn't actually resolve all issues especially those critical ones.

Being a people pleaser causes you to sacrifice being objective and truthful. Here the importance is on peoples' points of view, their emotions toward you as well, and not on the facts in which the work or task will be all about. Leaders find it difficult to work with such persons because they expect truthfulness from everyone when it comes to professional work. When all responsibilities are being agreed upon without the notion of actually accomplishing that work, leaders would find it stressful to meet deadlines and to delegate tasks again. However, this could be resolved. Know first the pattern of attitude and habits of a people pleaser, try to understand them and adjust for them since you only have the power to control your actions and not your subordinates or colleagues. As much as possible, try not to believe in everything that they say they can and will do. Make some adjustments for these people pleasers.

Over Promises, Never Delivers

Doesn't it stress you when someone overly promises and makes you believe he's actually capable of being trusted with tasks?

In the workplace, in relation to responsibilities and tasks, making promises is quite a crucial thing to do. For example, you have a team deadline to accomplish a certain report by the end of the week. Since he is also a people pleaser he agrees to take part of a certain part of the report. When asked whether he can accomplish the task right on time, he doesn't just agree on it but also promises a lot of things that will make you believe that he is certain to do it. The week passes and still no results. What would you feel as a leader? Aside from the stress you would be experiencing, you would be certainly pissed off. Why make any promises if you can't do the job right? Why can't he just be truthful about it, so that the task may be delegated to others? But that's the case with the super agreeable. It doesn't matter how many promises they make and how gravely it will affect the others as long as they will agree to it in the first place.

Unrealistic Commitments

Commitment is a deeper way of saying yes. Commitment indicates that no matter what happens, in anything that may come along your way, you will find a way for you to deliver the task.

For the super agreeable, it is easy for them to make such unrealistic commitments. Let's take the previous scenario, we showed above. What if, for example, instead of finishing the task after a week, he promises to finish it three days or two days later? Since the whole team knows how critical the work to be done is, they, including you as their leader, would not easily believe in it. Unrealistic as it may seem they would still continue to make such promises just to get your approval.

Avoids Conflicts at all costs

It is human nature to avoid conflict as far as is possible. The problem with these people pleasers is that they practically avoid every conflict that may arise and most of the time truthfulness is sacrificed. Going back to the same scenario we had, what if this super agreeable subordinate of yours do not really have the capacity to finish the work on time? Would it be a problem? In the mind of a super agreeable, every task delegated to him can result in a conflict if he does not agree to it. Set aside the other factors such as whether he could do it or not, his focus is on the avoiding negative results from others that could affect his emotions as well. Little did they know that by avoiding this conflict they are actually creating a bigger and more stressful conflict at the end of the day.

Always play safe

Playing-it-safe means creating invisible boundaries for your own advantage. The super agreeable tends to do such things for him to be able to deal harmoniously with this team or subordinates.

He maintains the level of responsibilities he can do without thinking of pushing his limits or working outside of his comfort zone.

Unable to say no

For some people, especially the super agreeable ones, rejecting others could be such a pain in the neck. Since this type of person wants to live harmoniously with everyone, saying no will create a negative feedback from them and it would not be a good idea. No matter what it is that is inside of a super agreeable, it doesn't matter, as long as he is asked if he could do something, he would answer yes without the assurance that he could actually accomplish it.

May be willing but lacks the potential

The super agreeable are sincere people. They may really want to help you but sometimes, but they lack the potential, capacity or resources to do so. No matter how good their intentions may be they cannot really deliver the help the other person needs if they is not totally capable of doing it. In the end it's not the intentions that matters, but the outcome of the work.

Coping strategies:

In appropriate situations and settings, encourage him to delegate more responsibilities to others especially in terms of critical tasks.

He may see this as a threat to his job, but if he does, explain that you really want to bring others into the picture because you know that he does a lot of work that no one can cover if he/she is absent and that can't be allowed to continue.

1. From time to time, maintain the habit of asking for feedback. Remind him that your approval of a certain matter is not dependent upon their agreement with you. Teaching people like this to argue their case is always going to be useful. It may be an idea to advise a person like this to become more defensive and there's no better way of explaining this than in a debating society. In one office where I worked, we had a debating society and always gave people pleasers the difficult topics so that they had to argue with others and could see the benefit of argument. These are people who are a little afraid of life. Help them to become stronger and they really are good workers. Allow them to continue to be people pleasers and you get nowhere.

2. Actively let him participate in the group's decision making activities. In that way he could talk more and you would let him exercise his thoughts more rather than simply listening and agreeing to what the others were saying. The debating society idea is a good one for training him/her to

speak up for themselves. In fact, they may have very creative ideas but are a little afraid to voice them.

3. Never forget to make him feel well respected through your choice of words and actions with regards to his opinions and work contributions. The people pleaser really does need this validation. If you show that you think they are needy, it will hurt them. Instead of doing this, make them feel valuable, but make sure that the work you give them is something that they are good at and can achieve fairly easily.

4. Be honest in every situation you would be dealing with him, including giving an honest appreciation and praise for all work well done. You might also want to ask his personal opinion regarding those things that could possibly interfere with your good working relationship and also be ready to negotiate if conflict ever arises.

5. Take time to give attention to his sense of humor. Sometimes, this type of person masks his true feelings through making fun of a situation. There may be hidden thoughts behind these humorous comments and you need to see the pattern. Often people pleasers use humor to hide real feelings. They kind of hide behind a mask. That mask protects them from getting hurt. I once asked an employee

Difficult People

why he used these tactics and although he was glib at first, he actually came to my office later in the day because he had a need to make me feel pleased with the outcome of our conversation. It turned out that he was always told that his opinion counted for nothing all of his life and so he stopped having one. If you find that you have a character such as this, who hides behind a mask because it's easier than being a failure, introduce things into the workplace that he is confident with and gradually increase the responsibility, building up the notion that he has worth. At the moment, he thinks he is worthless and doing this, you will have a very loyal member of staff at the end of it.

6. Let him know you accept him and find him a valuable person in the team. Try being personal. You can do this by remarking on his personal hobbies, good work habits, or even his family. You can do this without being phony, and also by meaning it sincerely even if these are brief conversations. This is what I did with the member of staff who was always joking with everyone. In truth, his life was so sad and the background behind his behavior was terrible. From childhood right through a miserable marriage, he had been rejected for being himself. It was never good enough, so he stopped being anyone and hid behind a mask because it was easier. Once they realize that

51

there is some good and that they do have value, people with low self-esteem can be taught to think in a different way. However, consistency is important to success. You can't be nice one minute and angry the next. You have to have a lot of patience and remember that you are fighting years of conditioning and that it will take time to break through that barrier.

7. Do not let them overcommit on any single task. Limit their work responsibilities. Do not let them take on more than they could handle and accomplish. Instead of making them do work that they know they will fail in, give them jobs you know they can excel in and congratulate them when they achieve, moving them onto more advanced jobs but making sure that you have sufficient time to teach them properly and go over the work with them so that they really can do the job without being supervised. That initial time put into training will really pay dividends.

8. Allow him to say no if the task is outside his capacity. Remind him that saying no is an option and that nobody is capable of doing everything. Point out to him the consequences of his decisions not just to him but also for the whole team. If you have a people pleaser in the office, these are difficult people to actually please. They seek

validation and they will continue to seek it. Make sure that validation is earned and give them jobs you know they can do so that you can rely upon the results.

9. Specify your work requests and time limits and be sure to tell everyone that these requests and time limits cannot be stretched under any circumstances. There are to be no excuses and those who feel they are unable to participate should feel free to say so.

The Chronic Complainer

"If you have time to whine and complain about something then you have the time to do something about it."

-Anthony J. D'Angelo

A chronic complainer finds endless reasons to moan about everything but doesn't have the initiative to act or resolve any of it. It's as if he was expecting that his act of complaining was the best way to solve the issue. Unconsciously, he is not aware that he likes having something to dislike and moan about. He is the type of person who finds fault in even the smallest of details. Sometimes, there are also people who we call creative faultfinders. They are people who find unattractive things to complain about to the extent that normal people don't seem to care at all if it does exist or not. This is the kind of person who spreads bad vibes.

On the other hand, occasions could arise when a so-called chronic complainer would find legitimate and justified concerns to whine about. However, there are those cases when such complainers would truly pull their weight to find a solution to his problems. Complainers are difficult because of the negativity that they spread and so need their activities stemmed as soon as possible.

According to Dr. Robert Bramson, author of the book, "Coping with Difficult People", repetitive complaints and grievances can cause people around the pathological complainer to become overly defensive. Most of the time, they tend to find a way to cordon themselves off to the negativity. Even if they do not admit it to themselves or the others around them, these complainers consider themselves perfect, prescriptive and also powerless. Due to this belief and thinking, time and effort eventually goes down the drain until the person becomes saddled with more problems to endure and worry about. They constantly think that no matter how they control the condition of their being powerless, they would not be able to solve and change things. Therefore, they would rather complain to those people who they think are able to get the work done. One distinct characteristic of difficult people is their being adamant to how things should work and any other contradiction to that would cause them to naturally complain.

Moreover, these types of people have a strong desire for perfection. Their attitude basically confirms their inability to have full control over a situation. Thus, this causes them to feel overly powerless, frustrated, and disenchanted. Despite the negative attributes of chronic complainer, it is still vital to consider this person as integral part of a group, department, and society in general. A good and effective leader knows how to bring the best out of his subordinates -- regardless of how difficult they can be.

Complainers bring productivity down. The reason for this is the negativity that they spread. People who are negative produce less work because they are less satisfied with the work environment because of the negativity. There are various ways to deal with complainers but it's best to try and seek the reason behind their negativity in the first place. If they think they are better than others, they need to understand that workplaces don't work well like that. They need to be taught empathy, being able to see things from other people's perspective and to learn respect for others.

Why is it not good to be a Chronic Complainer?

1. Psychologically and physically speaking, pessimism is not good for you.

2. Psychologist Martin Seligman concluded in his past research that those optimistic people are healthier, they live longer, enjoy life more, have more friends and better social lives, and are considered to be more successful at work.

3. Positive people tend to be more successful because they have the strong conviction and belief that they will achieve positive results in any task they exert effort to. The trouble with a complainer is that he/she does the opposite. They bring everyone into negative mode and that's bad news from the work point of view.

4. It can be contagious. It is not really a good thing that a small group can possibly be formed that has the common ground of the attitude of complaining. It could lead them to becoming overly critical of one another. I once worked in an office where we had one complainer. Whenever someone left the room, the complainer started to talk about that absent person. I noticed this was a habit and one day called her into my office to find out why she

needed to do this. Complainers are often not even aware that they are doing this. "Can you tell me please why you need to run people down when they are not there to defend themselves?" This was my question and the look that I got from her was one of incredulity. She could not believe that someone would ask a question like this. It transpired that she had very little to talk about and thought that this form of negativity was all she had to offer. We had employed a lot of younger women who were more modern in their approach and she found she had nothing in common with them. Listening to their preferences for TV shows where scandal was involved, she had evolved this system of getting into conversation by the back door, by being negative about people and spreading gossip. She needed friends and had none. We resolved this by telling her that a change of routine may help. I moved the desks around so that she was partnered with someone who she could relate to. She then found no reason to complain and seemed to change beyond recognition.

5. It promotes unhealthy professional relationships. Some people could unite and form a group based on common grievances, while others are compelled to join the same group out of disenchantment. However, professionalism is expected at all times in the workplace. This being said, an

employee should be keen on putting a barrier between professional issues and personal ones. When you find that personal problems are sneaking into the office, you need to put a stop to it straight away. In the front office of a real estate agency, I saw the worst kind of negativity. Two guys were arguing and demeaning each other in front of clients. As I listened to the conversation, I realized that their differences were personal ones and related to football. This is where the line needs to be drawn because if they are permitted to continue with negative interaction with each other, it's off-putting for clients and it makes clients think that there is no level of professionalism, meaning that they will look elsewhere.

6. It spreads negative vibes. It promotes negative ambiance in the workplace and can somehow affect work behavior. The working environment may turn out to be toxic one if the 'bad apples' are not managed well. If you are trying to be productive, there's nothing more off-putting than someone complaining in the background all the time. It sends the wrong message and it really kills the incentive to get things done.

7. It stops people from being innovative. Creativity and positivity could be compromised if such a person is a

chronic complainer. Instead of focusing more on how to streamline the processes and projects, he may be using his time more on things he feels so helpless about. Productivity of the individual and of the group may then suffer. If you see this happening, you have to stem it from the start because it upsets everyone. Even the complainer him/herself is not a happy person so you may be doing the complainer a service as well as others.

8. It discourages other people in the group. It can destroy all the positive vibes and hope that the group may have especially when dealing with a critical project. It demotivates people to take an active part in any task. Not only does complaining dampen team spirit and zap productivity as a whole, it also creates a sense of fear and apathy among group members. They expect the complaining. They go into meetings dreading the complaining and if you allow the workplace to be like this, you will never get productive meetings because of the attitude that even those who are great workers have is diminished to nothing by the negativity of the complainer.

9. The results you would be getting would be related to the thoughts you are most focusing on. The chronic complainer has this thing called confirmation bias.

According to Investopedia, confirmation bias is a psychological event that explains why certain people tend to voluntarily look for information that validates and coincides with their existing opinions. Someone suffering from this condition also tends to ignore information that is against their own opinion. It does affect perceptions, and more importantly, confirmation bias also leads to poor choices and decisions. If you find that a complainer is negatively impacting other staff, tell them that unless they are prepared to change, they will be placed in a job where they do not affect the performance of others.

10. Complaining can develop into an unwanted habit. The more you complain each day, the more negative you become, and eventually it will become a mindset which could be difficult to alter. If the person who complains does so to such an extent that it is becoming problematic not only to staff around them but to themselves, then it's time to suggest that they see a psychologist to discuss their problems. If they are negative to the point of affecting their own happiness as well as that of other people then they do need to know where professional lines are drawn. If you have someone that works in this field within the workplace, now may be a good time to send that employee to see them.

11. You tend to see the situation worse than it seems. People who complain a lot focus only on what's wrong. Even if good things were working out, they would still seek out negative things that they could complain about. The habit needs to be stemmed from the outset. Tell the complainer that he is affecting the morale of other workers and he will start to complain about that. Tell him that his behavior has to change or he will lose his job and he may stop for a while, but you need to keep on top of it because this is character type and he is likely to go back to negativity as part of who he is at some point in the future.

Steps on how to deal with complaints:

1. Ask specific questions that would be very informative and that could lead to solving the problems. Seek important facts and avoid unnecessary sayings. Be serious and put it in writing. Focus on getting precise information. If you are the complainer, then make sure that your complaints are not petty. If you are dealing with a complainer, then validity of the complaint has to be the first issue. If it is not valid, the complainer needs to be told that his complaining is wasting a lot of your time and needs to stop because it's affecting productivity and that can't happen.

2. Make an effort to listen. Aside from costing you nothing in listening, the more you focus and pay attention to the complainant, the more likely that you will resolve the situation. You may use physical signals and body languages to show that you are interested in what the other is saying and is actively listening. Remind yourself to take down important notes especially his critical point of interest. You may ask him to repeat what he was saying if you were not able to catch up. If the complainant is on the phone, you may want to ask your secretary or personal assistant to hold calls while you were dealing with an important matter. You may also invite the other person to meet you personally in order for you to communicate properly and more clearly. At the end of your conversation, you wrap things up by asking questions on how you can effectively address the complaint in a very friendly and respectful manner. Remember that at this point you are trying to resolve things in a friendly manner.

3. Show some sympathy. There would be times wherein you would not really agree with the complainant, but you have to remember that showing sympathy does not necessarily mean that you are wrong and that you are actually surrendering. The advantage in doing so is that you would be able to pacify the situation and make it easier for you to

think clearly about more important issues that are crucial in resolving the complaints. You could try saying these words like "that sounds difficult for you if I were in your shoes", or, "I'm really sorry to hear such things, I know there is something we could do" to show some sympathy and make him feel lighter regarding the situation. However, don't overplay the sympathy card because complainers who find someone who validates their complaints will return often to that person with more complaints.

4. Try not to justify first. Whatever the reason is, focus on obtaining a solution. The complainant is only after a solution and will likely ignore any reasoning you may have. Wrap up the conversation by asking the complainant how he wants to conclude the situation. This is a very wise move. "What do you suggest we do?" puts the ball into his court and he has to think of solutions. It's a very wise move because it will make him reticent to come to you with petty complaints, knowing that you will be asking him to try and find a way to resolve them.

William Lockhart

The Unresponsive Ones

The Silent and Quiet ones

This is the type of person who can extremely prudent with words to the point that they would rather not speak up in order for them to be safe and avoid any conflict. He tends to prioritize safety and limit risks by choosing not to respond or answer. Most of the time, these people are non-committal even if they are aware that something is not going right. They certainly avoid facing their fears by utilizing this type of mask called silence.

In the year 1993, Lewis-Ford, an organization dynamics teacher and management psychologist wrote in his work that this quiet and unresponsive type of person uses their silence as a weapon of defense just so they could easily avoid reproach and all the while hide their true selves. Practically speaking they were comparable to delinquent teens dodging some punishment after an unacceptable action done. However, they could also use their act of silence as a way to offend you and hurt you by concealing their true feelings.

This type of person can also be considered to be distrusting of others that can be the underlying reason why they always need to be on guard especially when speaking up and choosing the right set of words. Lewis-Ford further explains that maintaining the silence is also used as a way for them to avoid of reality. When they speak, they open up their hidden thoughts or horror, alarm, or panic-- anything that could be startling. This silence also can be used to hide their fear, anger, or it can also be a mean refusal to help or cooperate.

The association barriers they have established may cause them even bigger problems to deal with. Most of the time, they will not be very willing to talk to anyone openly. You will notice prolonged periods of silence when talking to them due to lack of faith and confidence in their lives and in themselves. This situation could result in torn communication lines and lasting relationship issues. A person who is classified as 'unresponsive' would usually demonstrate gestures or body language such as folding of arms, slouching, and even making growling sounds.

How to respond to the unresponsive ones effectively

1. Instead of exerting and wasting too much effort trying to decode what their silence really means, try to encourage them to open up and freely express themselves. Showing off a friendly smile in the first place, and letting them feel that you are the type of person that can be trusted could do this. Keep them in an environment that is conducive to interaction and communication. Take note of their body language and the moment they give the signal that they are

already comfortable and willing to speak up like for example simply returning a smile, an upright comfortable sitting position, and a focused eye contact then you should be ready to seize the moment and be able to listen well and maintain an open communication. Teaching them teamwork is also useful because if they are on a team with people that they trust they may be more likely to open up. The fact that they don't voice their opinions tells you that they are afraid of having their opinion made invalid by others. Choose a team carefully that you know will give him the encouragement that he craves.

2. In order for them to continue up speaking, ask open-ended questions. This will offer an opportunity for them to speak up their mind. Open ended questions are practically good and appropriate for these types of persons. They would tend to think more of what to say rather than leave the conversation hanging. With the trust they would give to you in the first place, it would not be good enough for them to stop thinking, talking and opening themselves up the more you show them how much interested you are in listening to them as well as thoroughly understanding what they say or mean.

3. Calmly wait for a response. Know the perfect timing on when the person is supposed to be the one to respond. Keep in mind that the purpose here is to let the silent person open up and you don't want to ruin your purpose by doing all the talking and not be able to wait for the other person to get his chance to speak. Do not also overwhelm him by being also silent. Try to keep up a good pace of communication in a well-balanced manner. As they say, timing is everything.

4. The use of counseling questions may also be a great tool to help improve the conversation. First of all, you have to be able to be aware of the problem for you to know the exact and right questions to be asked. Is this person really a silent and unresponsive one to everyone? Or he does only pick the people he would openly talk to? You must also be able to know some facts about him like his family or culture or his upbringing. In that way you would know the right approach you'd need for him. Try to further understand what he really means by what he is saying and try to read between the lines. Sometimes these people are ones who have the deepest thoughts to read and so try to be patient in understanding what they really mean. They could use different words to say one thing and you should

be able to keep up the pace of conversation to understand him better.

5. Try to avoid long pauses, awkward silence, and immense 'dead-air' in the conversation. As mentioned several times, silence is their comfort zone. And as much as you want them to open up for you, you may not want to invade their space too much. Try to make them feel at ease and wait for the right signals to talk. Let them keep up with the conversation and encourage them to speak more by asking questions. Look and sound interested, and stay focused, so that he may be able to show the same to you. Do not monopolize the discussion as it might also send a wrong message towards the other person.

6. Keep yourself composed and collected while waiting for your turn to talk. Waiting is essential here so as not to disrupt the other person's train of thought. The problem with the quiet person is that they already have a fear of speaking and if you interrupt, you are validating that fear. Let the silent person have a voice but let it be one that is heard and listened to.

7. Plan ahead and let the other person know that you are allotting a specific number of minutes for the conversation. Being aware of the time frame would enable

both parties to respect the turns and length of time in speaking. Encourage their input. "I really need to know what you feel about it" is an opener. "I don't have a lot of time, so please tell me what you think of the idea" is another that tells them that there is a time limitation that you are not prepared to go over.

8. In cases wherein you would unfortunately get no response at all, comment about the current situation and it with an open ended question. In that way, you could somehow encourage the other person to speak further.

9. Patience is a virtue. Therefore, be extra patient and try to wait as long as you can. Observe what is happening and then wait again. Be in control of the current interaction, particularly when he would try to say he doesn't know or try to leave the conversation.

10. If fortunately the situation lightens up and the other person has made an effort to open up, be more attentive and focused. Keep up with the tangential comments. They may actually lead you to something important and tangible. However, when the discussion has strayed away from the original topic, you may want to pull him back in and remind the person to stick to the original subject.

William Lockhart

In the scenario that they remain unable to speak and on guard, try to elude a polite ending. You may need to wrap up everything and end the meeting yourself and plan another one. And since a real discussion has not taken place yet, you should remind them of the objectives of the discussion.

If someone is really as quiet as this, how did they get past the interview? The chances are that they became like this for a reason. When you can ascertain what that reason is, you may find that they are silent in the workplace because someone has always shouted them down, so they don't feel free to discuss things. If this is the case, try to change people around so that they are separated from whoever is making them feel this way because this allows them to feel their problems are being addressed and that their views are being validated.

Shyness is a terrible thing. If you notice that someone is shy to the extent that they communicate very little with other workers, you need to develop a better relationship with them so that they feel more at ease about speaking. You may find that having social activities outside of work may be good for this type of employee. He/she may have particular interests. If you can find out what his/her passions are, you can work this into the work landscape so that you see that passionate side of his/her character sometimes. That's very good from a personnel point of view because others will be able to see that creative side too and are less likely to tease someone that they have become friends with outside of the work environment.

The Indecisive, the Ditherer, the Hesitant
Dealing with a waffler coworker

> *"Each indecision brings its own delays and days are lost lamenting over lost days ... What you can do or think you can do, begin it. For boldness has magic, power, and genius in it."*
>
> *Johann Wolfgang von Goethe (1749 - 1832)*

A waffler or an indecisive person may change his mind in an instant, and may even reverse his previous decision. In a fast-paced work environment, this type of person may drive his co-workers mad. A waffler has the tendency to disrupt an on-going task that could consequently lead to delays. These are the people who are unable to demonstrate their 'inner perfectionist selves. They want everything to be done perfectly and you will see that they get overly frustrated when things do not go their way.

According to Dr. Robert Bramson, people who suffer from this behavioral issue usually fall under two different categories. The first one would want things to be done his way or no way at all. For him, the only best thing he could get from the situation is that he could gain control of everything. This person does not believe in accountability. He wants to take control the situation but is unable to take in criticisms. Everything should go according to plan and be perfect. He does not want to belong to a group where his ideas are contradicted and questioned. He feels that his ideas are valid, but the problem is that his ideas keep changing and changing goal posts in a work situation are unhealthy for those people who have to take orders from him.

The other one is someone who, at times, would purposefully draw out discussions by introducing different point of views that can very well frustrate the remaining members of the group. They have way too many ideas that they tend to lose focus on what is essential. Most of the time, these people are known to be 'scatter brains.' These people are not equipped with the skills to present their ideas systematically. The lack of organization may result in conflicts among the group members. In fact, during the course of a meeting, a person of this nature can switch subjects so many times that you lose touch with the purpose of the meeting in the first place.

This person can also be concluded not to be good at communicating his own thoughts because of this idea. His needs and opinions are also affected as he finds it difficult to share it to others around him. These people are expected to slow down to be able to cope with the accumulating stress and pressure coming from the other people of the group. They are better placed in a job which is not that interactive with others and where they can get on with their work and know what that work entails.

In dealing with the stress, they tend to procrastinate unconsciously without being aware that they are already bringing other people in the workplace down and that they are not being very helpful at all. They put many tasks on halt without taking into consideration the impact it has on the project and on the group. As a result, those who are on the receiving end of the indecisiveness lose their excitement and also the existing commitment to the project or to the person that would also bring down the group. Although they may succeed in dodging the decision, this person would still be stressed over the amount of tension the situation has caused.

Given all these facts, it does not necessarily mean that they are not able to take and make decisions, and to take part in an effective communication. They also usually talk in short, concise and may use very limited phrases or sentences. They demonstrate the body language of a typical person lacking the confidence to make decisions. Unfortunately, due to the frustration that his co-workers get from the lack of communication, this indecisive person gets ignored or cordoned off, and their limited words seem not to matter at all.

They can also be very sensitive and could withhold essential information and ideas because they would first worry about how it will be accepted, understood and perceived by his group or the person who need it. Chances are, if they think that the information they have is not too critical and valuable, they would also feel that the same does for their opinions and so they would rather not decide to tell it at all because someone else could deal with it anyway.

How to communicate well with a waffler:

1. Try to lighten up the mood during the conversation. Make it easy for him to tell you about things or reasons that directly affect him when making and implementing a decision. Try to interpret his thoughts while he is explaining his unorganized thoughts. Through his words, try to sort out his and ideas and look for material information you might need. Study his words and try to understand the reason behind his being so reserved with all his ideas and actions.

2. Listen for roundabout words and exclusions that may give pieces of information about a specific issue. Most people, like Dr. Bramson said, do not place attention on these small details. However, since you are trying to solve the issue, you must avoid dwelling on the small unnecessary

Difficult People

details. Look at the actual problem and deal with it. These words could very well help you in achieving a successful conversation with a waffler.

3. When you have finally get to the real issue, help them tackle this by presenting them with viable options. Always remember that the purpose here is to come up with the ultimate decision. So, if you think your conversation is slowly nearing to that end goal, you might as well help him get there by clearing out unnecessary thoughts and organizing ideas that he already has.

4. At some point, their reservations will speak the truth for you. Assuming this is the case, recognize any past issues and state pertinent information without being defensive. Propose an arrangement and request for help. Be mindful that you have to be sensitive with their feelings and emotions so that you avoid the other person from shutting him down and eventually ruin the conversation. Try to limit your talk in this part and encourage him to open up himself. Think of better ways to seek help from him in order to achieve the purpose of your conversation. I remember working with someone like this who could not keep on topic at all. They jumped from subject to subject until you no longer knew what the reason for the meeting

was any more. We tackled it by having a set agenda. If anyone brought anything up that was not on the agenda it was quashed. It's as simple as that.

5. Further inspect the actualities even if you are not getting any relevant information from the conversation. Look into the problem by probing or by analyzing any information you have at the moment. Remember to give priority to existing actual facts and consider them as well. This will continuously offer you thoughts to ponder on. Being sensitive to any given information would essentially help you sort the problem with the waffler.

6. Be firm in stressing the importance and quality and service of your proposition. Help him understand the purpose of your project.

7. Express appreciation every time this person cooperates with you. If the person has become particularly helpful in attaining a task, give him credit and express your gratitude. Know that these people find it extremely difficult to participate in any project or task actively. Therefore, any contribution would mean that the person truly exerted some genuine efforts.

8.

9. Be keen on writing the progress on a journal. This could serve as a good reference should you experience the same problem in the future.

Your sensitivity can be your ultimate tool in dealing with this type of difficult people. Looking at the situation from different perspectives and utilizing the right amount of patience can help you withstand the pressure and the tension from working with difficult individuals.

The Negative

> "A pessimist is a man who thinks everybody is as nasty as himself, and hates them for it" – George Bernard Shaw

Pessimistic individuals can genuinely act as the *'party pooper'* in any discussion. They aren't the most charming individuals to be around with. Regardless of what you say, they have a method for turning things around and they seem negative, hopeless, and helpless. Some antagonistic individuals can be negative to the point that it feels depleting simply being around them.

A negative co-worker is one of the most influential persons in a workplace. He always expects the worst outcome from a certain project or work may lead to perfection and that it could prevent a lot of disappointments among the group. It may sound good at

William Lockhart

first till you witness how the pessimistic works with others in the process of doing such project.

The Negativist is best depicted as an identity that not just opposes ideas, but also contributes to the worsening of any projects or plans. Being negativist means that a person is someone who keeps himself focused what is worst to happen or what more is lacking for a certain project. Also, a pessimistic person never fails to remind his group of the numerous failures they have encountered.

He will always interrupt the group by criticizing every outcome, yet he won't give any good suggestions on improvising what he just criticized. Negativists don't just focus on the outcomes to criticize. One of the traits a negativist has is his ability directly criticize his co-workers. Whatever you say, he can find many different reasons to back up his viewpoint. The discussion will just swirl into more negativity, and everyone in the workplace will just pull themselves down in the process. They can give constructive comments, but a negativist will always rebuts with no signs of backing down.

Productivity can plummet when someone with overflowing pessimism has infiltrated a group. Nothing good can also come out of debating with such person. Also, it will absolutely lead to a larger gap in terms of relationship among the colleagues. Failure to work with your co-workers in harmony is one of the most common distractions that could hamper any accomplishment in the workplace.

While negativist's feedback could be translated as useful, it may still upset the other members of the group. The problem could escalate and even cause problems on the working relationships insider the office. Another regular reference to the negativist is the doubter. Like the negativist these people like to shred and shoot gaps in whatever is being said right now. They destroy their appreciated after some time as individuals get on to their interminable pessimism.

Inside the character of a man why should considered be negative is an individual who is experiencing issues managing a profound situated internal clash. This more often than not originates from an inclination that they don't have power over their own lives. The negativist is not able to work through essential human frustration. A negativist accepts that everybody can relate also, comprehend the well of baffle they feel towards humankind and our own particular flaw.

While these individuals are so staggeringly disillusioned about existence and how it treats them, they are equipped for having profound individual feelings at any undertaking that is set before them. In any case, on the off chance that they are not in direct control of the venture, it will come up short in light of the fact that they accept that nobody can handle or perform an assignment truly like they can.

Why is it not good to be a Negativist?
1. Negativists are not good at self-feedback. Self-feedback causes a downward spiral of low self- esteem, which can be particularly bad in any workplace.

2. Negativists strongly believe that problematic situations are lasting, almost permanent. They accept that great occasions are just temporary. That is preventing them to fully enjoy and cherish every moment in their lives and just drowns themselves thinking about those negative thoughts. Negative thoughts eventually become a way of life for them.

3. Negativists accept that despondency is typical and great things are brought about by particular occasions. This makes it easy for them to absorb negative thoughts and repel those that appear pleasant.

4. Negativists accept that awful occasions are their deficiency. However, once in a while, things simply happen to turn out well. It always turns them down that a

certain project in a group where they belong turns out to be a failure. It makes them more and more pessimist.

5. It will lead you to undesirable future. Your present activities build up on your future. Your misery will escalate if you fail to get rid of the pessimism you deal with on a daily basis. The more you gripe, the more things you will discover to whine about.

6. Pessimism shortens your life span. The longer and the more you live an irate life, the shorter your lifespan is. Your negative thoughts can accumulate until you become physically ill and eventually plagued with a disease. Before you know it, you would face the biggest turmoil of your life -- and it would be too late.

7. Obviously, negativism produces negative outcomes. This is one of the most obvious impacts of dwelling on negative thoughts. For the most part individuals believe it's the other route round, yet that is not the situation. Your reasoning causes your circumstances.

8. Pessimistic people tend to harm others. Your negative mindset influences individuals around you. You ought to never make others feel awful as you would only be

contributing to your own hopelessness, as well as to the despondency of others.

Dealing with the pessimists:

1. Your organization society is detrimental to your image. One 'bad apple' in the bunch can instantly influence the whole culture of your business. As they say, it only takes a single bad apple to spoil the entire bunch. This means that effective management of the person and how he deals with others is of paramount importance. The speedier you manage a negative associate, the faster you will have the capacity to gauge the situation. Have a meeting, pass on your worries and allow the individual to change. To weed out this particular source of negativity would be beneficial to the entire society.

2. Be realistic rather than idealistic when it comes to dealing with someone who is overly negative. Understand his frame of mind and be strategic as well.

3. Distance works. Avoid them. Individuals who gripe about everything will never improve your life. They don't offer real solutions but are only keen on drawing the attention to themselves. They will suck your energy out and will make you dwell on their own negative realm as well. When

you get the chance to avoid them, do so. You are better off alone rather than being surrounded by people who do not do good in your life.

4. Don't argue with them, as they will not listen anyway. Arguing would only deepen the curs in the work relationships you have. Distance and silence still remain the best solutions in dealing with these kinds of people.

5. Be positive towards them. Your bliss and wellbeing are excessively essential in protecting yourself, making it impossible for anyone to influence you in a negative manner. Stay positive and start to restrain your time with the negative people throughout your life. Your positive attitude will serve as their Achilles' heel. Your strength is ultimately their weakness.

6. Try not to offer any options yourself until the issue has been completely examined. Exert effort to understand the situation better and this will give you a hand in making sound decisions that involve these people.

7. Don't exaggerate every situation you deal with a pessimist. Negative individuals can once in a while carry on nonsensically. You will squander significant time and vitality in the event that you attempt to comprehend their

activities. Do whatever you can to keep yourself from turning out to be candidly put resources into their issues.

8. Build your own support group. Establish a circle of positive companions, associates and expert contacts. When somebody discovers how to get under your skin, you will be unable to deal with the circumstance independent from anyone else. Know and acknowledge when you need help. Get one. When you discover yourself turning out to be excessively enthusiastic, call a companion or coach and to check your condition. Be vigilant in choosing your companion and communicate to them as often as possible.

9. Be aware of the huge possibility that you can also get trapped in despondency if you fail to screen the people you spend time with on a daily basis. Consider this as a potential weakness, and prepare for a battle.

10. You should set your boundaries and establish barriers when necessary. Try not to feel forced to sit down and listen to an individual who is only after your attention and nothing else. Their negative vitality will saturate your own life and influence your demeanor. Set points of confinement and put some separation in the middle of yourself and this person. On the circumstance that you must relate yourself with an adverse individual do

remember to keep your cooperation short. You can't control the negative conduct, however you can control regardless of whether you lock in.

11. Try not to give in every time somebody aggravates you. You may be provoked at some point but learn how to brush it off. Leave pointless clash. Be the bigger person and leave any unnecessary discussion with someone who is perceived as negative. You first actions can either save you or break you. It is up to you on how you can protect yourself more from these kinds of people.

12. Finally, be prepared to make a move on your own. Be honest enough to make people know what you are up to. Your transparency could encourage negative people to be more open and honest with you as well.

If you find that their negativity is really affecting your attitude toward work, tell them. It may seem a little harsh but much of the time, they don't know how much they are affecting other people. I worked with one person who was very critical of everything within the workplace to such an extent that he actually had people believing the things he was saying although they were unfounded. Snide little comments like "If you had the experience of this company that I have..." were enough to make the gullible believe in what he was saying. However, the best way of dealing with this is not in private. It's to have a meeting that includes everybody – negative and positive – and not single out a single person as being the cause of negativity. Ask for people to get their grievances out in public so that they can be addressed. Once they are, you may find that the negative person goes back to being normal for a while, although don't expect a leopard to change his spots overnight.

If you get feedback through the grapevine that he has started again, then something needs to be done and you need to talk about negative attitude in the workplace and what it does to erode the productivity of the place. Introduce goals, introduce goals that are achievable with hard work and what you do is increase competition within the workplace. The person who is too busy being pessimistic won't keep those deadlines, but people will be proud of those who do. The whiner needs to understand that whining does not receive any awards and that it's not in the interests of anyone to continue to see the cup as half empty.

The Aggressive and Offensive

"Gentleness corrects whatever is offensive in our manner."

-Hugh Blair

"It's one thing to say, 'I don't like what you said to me and I find it rude and offensive,' but the moment you threaten

violence in return, you've taken it to another level, where you lose whatever credibility you had."

-Salman Rushdie

There are many names you may call these offensive ones. They may be control freaks, hostile, bullies, aggressive, and belligerent.

Back in the year 1988, Dr. Robert Bramson metaphorically identified these types of people into three categories: The Sherman Tank, The Sniper, and The Exploder.

The Sherman Tank

The core belief and of this person is "If I can make you look powerless, wavering, or ambiguous, then I will appear, to myself as well as other people, solid beyond any doubt."

The use of the metaphor Sherman tank perfectly depicts what a hostile person actually does. They turn out charging. They are oppressive, intimidating, and overpowering. They assault individual behaviors and even personal characteristics. They further attack you with unwavering reactions and arguments. Sherman Tanks ordinarily accomplish their short-run targets, yet at the expense of lost companionship, and long haul of broken connections. They make themselves look better at the expense of others.

Sherman Tanks have a compelling need to demonstrate to themselves as well as other people that their perspective of the world is correct. They have an intense feeling of how others ought to act, and they are not hesitant to let them know about it. They also do prioritize and give importance to confidence and aggressiveness that causes them to undermine those people around them who they think do not possess those qualities.

How to deal with a Sherman Tank

    a. Use your friendliness to your advantage. Try to make a pleasant atmosphere for both of you. Show him good attitude and remarks that would somehow encourage him to do the same. Demonstrate how to speak well with sensitivity. Let him know that you are conversing with him as a friend and not as a foe. Make him feel that you genuinely care for him. Maintain a harmonious flow of conversation and do not forget that you are not just talking as co-workers but people who are concerned with each other not just only regarding a project or work. Being friendly towards a Sherman Tank doesn't mean that you are lowering your guard and your pride or even scooping down to his level, it would only mean that you value your peace and harmonious work relationship rather than sticking solely to facts never minding offending anyone.

b. In the middle of your conversation do not try to cut down whatever they are saying even if you are tempted to. Moreover, do not also try to start a debate on his point. In some or most cases you would find this Sherman Tank to be pointless with no facts to back up his words but only rudeness and arrogance, however, try to listen well and hold back your tongue to prevent tension in between your conversation. Always remember to know your timing in speaking and defending your thoughts. Not cutting him off during his talk doesn't mean you believe in him, it is just a matter of respect on the other person in which you are implying to expect the same.

c. Be keen on stating your own opinions. The moment the right timing comes and the Sherman Tank already finished his statement it's now time to move on to your side and make him willingly listen to you and understand the facts that you are presenting to him. Remember that in this situation, he will be the receiver of ideas and while you value respect and right timing this person may not value the same thing as you do an may offend you at the middle of your talk. When this thing happen try to maintain your calm and patience and stick to your facts.

d. Keep your eye contact with the Sherman Tank. Show him that you are paying enough attention and interest that he should also do the same. Pay due respect to the other person even if you do not feel like doing so. Maintaining eye contact with this person may be crucial especially in between the conversation wherein you may find him offensive, however, doing so helps you lower his actions of rudeness by creating a sensitive atmosphere showing him you are a person with emotions and that his verbal actions may not be healthy for the both of you.

e. Getting him to sit down is a nice way to keep the situation better. A good posture during a conversation is always a big factor, including how comfortable the person regarding the atmosphere and the environment. A nice, cozy, and not so noisy place could be a good factor in order for you to have a well formed conversation with this person.

f. Grab his attention and see to it that he focuses on you, not only by keeping your eye contact but also by also consistently calling him by name. It makes your conversation more personal and more comfortable with the Sherman Tank. Unconsciously make this person like talking to you. This way you could lower down his aggressiveness and may even be nice talking to you.

g. While we value being respectful all throughout the conversation, remember to get in any way that you can to expose your thoughts especially if the person is really getting difficult in letting you finish your sentences. Make him respect you as well. As for you, you must first believe and be consistent on your ideas so that he may be compelled to believe in what you are saying.

h. Most importantly, let the Sherman Tank breathe and cool down by giving him time to run down. Oftentimes, this person unconsciously finds himself tired and pressured of his own talk. Make him feel relax and comfortable with you and with the situation.

The Sniper

Much like the Sherman Tank, Snipers strongly believe that making others look terrible makes themselves look great. They likewise have an intense feeling of what others ought to be doing. However, their consistent cutting comments for the most part demotivate co-workers instead of promoting results. If the sniper has you in his target, then watch out because he won't stop until he achieves demoralizing you.

Contrary to the Sherman Tank, these snipers prefers a more secure, refine and that they are somewhat more conservative by nature. They may appear nice and even overly caring on the outside. However, they can do mean things behind your back. They tend to attack you when you least expect it. They make sure that they get to you every time they do something. They find joy in making your life just as miserable. Worse, these people do not demonstrate remorse when huge damage has been done. They would use social barriers in order for them to form a secured place from which to attack out at targets of resentment or envy.

They combine their verbal rockets with non-verbal signs of liveliness and kinship. This makes a circumstance where any striking back at the sniper can be seen as a forceful demonstration, similar to you doing the assaulting not the protecting.

Howto deal with a Sniper

    a. In the event that you are just a witness to a circumstance with a Sniper, stay out of it, yet demand that it stops before you. Same with dealing with a Sherman Tank, make him feel that you must be respected and that he should show the same to the other people in the workplace. Imply that he should be sensitive enough to others' feelings especially in the workplace where all persons should act professionally and with acts of maturity.

b. Planning and executing regular meetings focused mainly on problem solving could also lessen the possibility of persons in your workplace to do certain sniping. Help out in shifting their plans. Make them involve in activities and keep them busy. This would lessen their chance of 'planning' an attack against a target.

c. As timing is very important in every circumstance, please bear in mind that you need and are expected to act as fast as you can in solving problems that may arise in relation to person in your workplace that is a Sniper. Dealing with this kind of person should be act upon as early as you can because it may affect other persons in your group or even the work itself that you can no longer control if you did not act as early as the beginning of the issue.

d. Try to always look at the bigger picture involving the other people in your group and their ideas as well. Focus on what would really help figure out the situation or the work that you are dealing on. Try to shove negative vibes especially on group meetings wherein you should act seriously and professionally. Do your best not to be swayed by emotions in which the sniper may be targeting you.

e. Give them a distinct option for an immediate challenge. As the Sniper is somehow arrogant, shift their negative side as a positive one for the benefit of the whole group. Make his words a direct attack on himself on which he may be surprised to be a difficult encounter for him. Make him act on everything that he says.

f. Given all these, remember not to let these people affect you and your plans. Dealing with a sniper could be difficult but with the right attitude and patience you could smoke out a sniper all the while not letting social tradition stop you.

The Exploder

Exploders are characterized by attacks of fierceness, fueling assaults that appear to be rarely under control.

Dr. Bramson noted that these fits of rage could eject out of discussions and dialogs that appear to begin as cordial. Generally these fits happen when the exploder feels physically or mentally undermined. Much of the time an Exploder's reaction to a debilitating comment is first outrage followed by either accusing or suspicion.

How to deal with an Exploder

a. If it is at all possible, bring a breather, the one who could patiently handle and control the situation without getting mad, to the Exploder and privately settle the circumstance without anyone getting involved that could just worsen the matters. You need to handle the exploder with kid gloves.

b. The same with handling all the Sherman Tank and the Sniper, make it known to him that you don't make fun of him and that you take him seriously as well the situation you are dealing with. Showing interest with this person could lessen the probability that he will continue the same bad attitude towards you.

In the event that they still could not control themselves, their temper and tantrums, cut them with a neutral remark like saying 'Stop'. This way he will be reminded that what he is doing is already wrong and that he literally needs to stop.

William Lockhart

Chapter 3
How to Deal with Difficult People?

There are few measures that can help to deal with challenging people and also improve their behavior. The trick lies in being calm and patient, yet staying on a firm ground. It should also be kept in mind that most of the times the problem is just a perception issue. You might be difficult for the person who is difficult for you.

Before branding someone as problematic, check that there is no problem from your side. For example: some people are introvert and might irritate the ones who are very social, this doesn't mean that they have a difficult nature. They just have opposite personality with respect to the extrovert people and therefore might face problems with them.

Reforming Steps

Here are the steps by which you can bring a change in the behavior of difficult people:

- The first point to realize is that it's the "difficult trait" that is troublesome and not the person in general. It is just like teaching a student or correcting a child. When children commit a mistake, you scold them for the mistake and not bash them completely. When we realize that the person might be really good and sincere and only has a problematic character, facing them becomes easier and we automatically develop patience enough to stand them.

- If the person is close to you then it's better to tell them directly about their nature instead of beating around the bush. Don't bring this topic in a tensed situation or in an argument. Anger makes us say a lot of things that are not true and might hurt the other person a lot. Acceptance of others' views also becomes difficult when we are agitated. Bring out this topic when you both are relaxed and calm. Don't be vague in your remarks. Tell the person specifically the things that are disturbing and if possible cite them with examples. Tell them that you are doing this for their better future and it would benefit them when they interact with new people in foreign place where they would not have any kind of family support.

- Immediately ask them for a feedback. If you go on and on, it might seem like you are just ranting and the person might not take your advice seriously. Ask their opinion time to time and if they don't agree to you, ask them the reason. They might also get defensive and start picking out flaws in your nature. Be prepared for such situations and accept your mistakes wherever you find the person to be correct. If you completely deny everything the person says there are chances he or she might not listen to you. Be open to yourself and slowly they'll also open up to you.

- Avoid getting agitated while explaining things to them. Most probably they will reject your notion the first time, don't lose your cool in such cases. Be firm yet polite and don't lose your focus from the topic. It becomes easy to stray when we are highly emotional and it can lead to more conflicts. Instead, avoid giving in to any kind of negative emotion if the person is showing resistance to your views. Eventually they will realize that the actual problem lies with them.

Survival Steps

If you have tried every way to help the difficult person but still nothing is working out, you might as well as stick to easy survival with such people. Often we encounter strangers and colleagues who are not really close to us; in such cases also it is better to learn to deal with them than improve their behavior. Here are the ways by which you can manage staying around difficult people:

- Avoid crossing paths with them as much as possible. If you study in the same institution, keep the conversation limited to academics. If it's a workplace, avoid lunching with them and restrict your meetings to only work related assemblies. It might appear as backing off, but in long run this is going to be beneficial to both of you. It is not always good to start a fight as it can rob you of your mental piece and can affect your personal life too. Until and unless the person is not harming you in any way, avoid getting into a conflict and maintain a distance.

- Predict their actions beforehand and work accordingly. For example: if you know that a person has a habit of rejecting others' ideas, ask them first for the ideas. When they have finally said what they want, give your input and correct them wherever you feel it is required.

Mention it beforehand formally that you both have to listen to each other without interruption first and then give inputs.

- Be the first one to end the conversation. If you have been dragged into conversing with a demanding person, find ways to end it as quickly and swiftly as possible. For example: if you encounter someone who just advices people constantly and finds flaws in their work, reply "Thank you" and just end the conversation. Trying to justify to such a person will only lead to an accelerated discussion. If you are around someone who constantly brags, don't ask them questions or try to taunt them when they are bragging. Instead a simple "I am glad" or "Good for you" with a smile will make them stop.

- Keep in mind to maintain your calm all the time when dealing with such people. In a fit of rage and irritation, don't act foolishly. If it is getting to hard to manage, tell them politely that you want to keep a certain distance from them. The relationship might change between you two after this statement, but it is still better than confronting mean behavior on a daily basis. If the relationship means a lot to you, the situation will not reach at this point to begin with. Remember, stressful relationships always hamper our progress in the end, be it with a friend or a colleague or even with a boss.

How to define difficult

This question is one that workplace psychologists find the most difficult to answer because different things annoy different types of people. What you need to ask yourself is whether someone, in the workplace, is making your working life disagreeable. Then, having pinpointed that, you also need to work out in what way they are making your life difficult. Sometimes an adjustment of your attitude changes the dynamics of the situation. Perhaps it's you who is sensitive. I knew a woman who had gone through her career jumping from one seemingly good job to another but on a parallel. She was never working her way up the chain – always across and she always left a situation because others within the workplace annoyed her. What she didn't see was that it was the way she interacted with others that others found annoying. She was not popular. She was not empathetic, had no time for niceties and simply used the work environment to earn money. You may say we all do, but in her case, it was more than that. She didn't want any personal contact with anyone and when people made the move to be friendly, she actually turned on them and made them hostile. She had not seen that she was the problem or that the reason people continually rejected her was her own behavior.

If there are people within the workplace that are difficult, you need to examine exactly why. For instance, I could mention people within the span of my career who I found to be very negative to my career path. These are instances that I can cite:

- A boss who took the credit for my work
- A boss who didn't trust me enough to let me do things
- A colleague who mocked the fact that I wasn't young
- Colleagues that ganged up together and made fun of people
- The bully
- The office Romeo
- The physical abuser
- The mental abuser

These are all types of people that I have had to deal with in the course of my career. To make it clear to myself that it wasn't me that was at fault, I analyzed each situation before deciding what my career move would be. Let us go through some of this because it will show you how to evaluate the situation and decide upon the acceptability of the behaviors being shown toward you.

The boss who took credit for my work

In this situation, everyone wants to be the hero. Occasional taking of credit is okay. It's kind of to be expected. You work for a team, you come up with a wonderful suggestion that revolutionizes the way that your place of work functions. Basically, you can say that you are one of a team. That team works under a boss who is accountable to a boss. When he reports to the boss, he comes up with a report showing the boss what his team have come up with. Often, your boss doesn't give credit to individuals. He will give credit to the team. That's normal. Everyone takes the credit for working together.

However, if you have a boss that takes your ideas and passes them off as his own, then that's another thing altogether. In this situation, your boss is lying. I had one boss that did this and it hurt my feelings that I was getting absolutely no credit for the things that I was doing. It was a well-paid job and I loved it except for this one small detail. If my boss gave me no credit, it wasn't going on my work record and was thus not going to help me in my plight to gain promotion. I needed his recognition of my skills. I decided to tackle this head on by talking in private to him. When you talk behind people's backs, you may think that everyone agrees with you to your face. However, it doesn't help the situation and can make the distance between you and the boss even worse. I decided that the problem was between him and me and that this should be the limit of the discussions.

I explained about the ideas that I had come up with which he knew to be fact and told him that I was unhappy about the fact that my part in those decisions was not acknowledged. I further told him that if this was to continue, then I saw no reason to come up with creative ideas that helped the place. He was effectively backed into a corner. I told him that while I was prepared to let the past sins go, I wasn't going to do that on an ongoing basis. He knew that I was carrying him and that without my support, he really didn't have much of a clue. I had done this for too long. I also told him that I liked him very much as a boss and that this was my only gripe against him and he could see where it was coming from.

Over the course of the next year, my career took off but he called me into his office one day to talk to me. He had taken credit because he was afraid of losing me from the team. If the people higher up recognized my skills, the chances are that he would have had to take on a rookie and he really didn't want to do that when I was so good at my job. He admitted to holding me back in my career. You forge a kind of solidarity when you are honest with people and can keep all of your negotiations on an honest level without having to bandy about insults. Keep your facts straight. Don't let emotions into the issue and you will find solutions that work for everyone. We did. My ideas were put forward as my ideas from then on and although that gained me pay rise after pay rise, I didn't take the bait when offered a placement in a new office because I actually liked being where I was and was earning good money. By listening to my complaint and taking it aboard, I was able to stem the behavior of my boss and start a relationship which was on an equal footing without having all the baggage of resentment.

The boss who didn't trust me enough to do things

If you have a boss like this, perhaps he is a perfectionist. This boss annoyed me to the point of wanting to throw things at him and I am a very mild mannered person. He would give me a job to do and then every half hour or so would come to my desk and try to do the job himself. He wasted my time, he did not recognize my ability and was making my working life an absolute nightmare. In the end, there was no other way to deal with this boss than to take all the files and to ceremoniously dump them onto his desk with the following speech.

"If you don't trust me enough to do something alone, then I cannot continue to work for you. I am a competent qualified person and every job you give me, you drive me nuts by checking on me every five minutes as if I have no ability at all. If you don't trust coworkers, you will lose them because they need that trust. When you are ready to trust me, give the files back."

The man was speechless but I don't think that he had realized the error of his ways before that moment in time. He was a helpful kind of guy and was trying to give me all the backup that he thought I needed, but had no sense of delegation. Bosses who cannot delegate are the worst type to have. They dabble at delegation but they hold onto the work they have delegated because they are friendly and helpful and a little perfectionist in the way that they deal with work. No one does it as good as they do. Therefore, they are drawn to helping all of the time and show no trust in their staff.

A colleague who mocked that I was no longer young

Although you may not see this as a problem in the workplace, it can become one if you have too much diversity in the age range of employees. Progress tends to leave older people behind and it can make them feel used up and have a very bitter outlook. In my case, that didn't happen because I had enough confidence in my own ability to deal with it, although I have seen the mockery of younger staff geared toward older staff and this really can play havoc in the workplace. Staff who do this need to be told that the older members of staff are equally as important. Involve them in meetings. Use their expertise and let younger members of staff deal with modern elements such as social media. There is actually a valid place for everyone within the workplace and younger people teasing older members of staff is not acceptable.

Perhaps the older members of staff have been with the company for a long time and have a history. They know the company back to front and inside out and although they may not have learned new ways, they are every bit as valid and have some kind of loyalty to the company. The company should therefore have some kind of loyalty to them.

Colleagues that ganged up together and made fun of people

If this is the way that staff deals with each other, it isn't pleasant. I have walked into offices where people snigger. They may have a problem because someone isn't fashionable enough, or different in some way, but there is a reason why the company is employing that person and this should be remembered. In fact, I remember experiencing this and finding it very petty when targeted against someone who had a problem with acne. It was positively unkind. The way that the boss dealt with it was a very good way because he drew attention to each of the defects of those who were scorning others and asked how they would feel if they thought that the board of directors was sniggling behind their backs about their shortcomings. He took all of the members of staff who were indulging in this behavior to one side and explained that it was making the work environment difficult for people who had more respect.

Two of the people involved were the gang leaders. In order to deal with this, he moved one to another floor of the building so that she was still working for the company but was unable to influence the other. The other person on her own was not so good at bullying and many bullies depend upon a crowd or stronger persons to egg them on. The situation vastly improved for everyone. It's unkind to be nasty to other members of staff. I have experienced this in several workplaces. People were treated differently for various reasons and these include:

- Race

- Sexual orientation

- The way that they dressed

- The way that they talked

- Whether the gang thought they were the boss's favorite

When shove comes to push, people usually behave in this manner when they are outside of their comfort zone and want to hide their own insecurities and weakness. Bullies tend to be people who have been bullied. They feel that the only way that they can avoid that bullying is to behave in that way toward others. It isn't and cannot be tolerated.

The Office Romeo

Romance within the workplace should be avoided if at all possible, though when you mix men and women within a workplace, expect fireworks. The fact is that people spend a lot of time at work and relationships form. It's good to have a "no relationships with colleagues" policy as this puts people off the idea of romancing people they work with. However, the office Romeo is something else. He is the guy that always chats up new staff members. He's the one who runs to get her coffee or meets her in the canteen. He's done it time and time again and will no doubt end up breaking her heart. It's a little like in the real world except that this guy thinks he is the king pin and will continue to try and impress his colleagues with his success rate.

If there is someone that fits this description within the workplace, be careful because the disruption that this can cause among staff really can be negative. Having ditched one girl, he then chats up another and there becomes a situation where there is jealousy, anger, resentment and where emotions are being played with. A warning would be in order if he were a habitual Romeo. Of course, there are genuine people who meet and fall in love within the workplace but this is a very different story. The Romeo is a serial relationship maker and breaker and will use his charms to get what he wants. He loves the unobtainable and will go out of his way to get it, casting it aside once he has achieved his aims.

The physical abuser

You may think that you would have to go back to the dark ages to find someone who actually abuses colleagues, but you would be wrong. In a sweatshop situation, those who are abused are afraid and succumb to abuse because their fear is so great of losing their jobs. Often you find this mentality of person in a situation where you have one main controller and many women working for him. A shop, a factory or an office can have someone of this nature and if someone has physically hurt you, you need to voice your opinion and tell someone. Often, in situations such as this, there is no one that the victim can turn to. Who do you tell when your boss is expecting to have sexual favors? He is the one that decides your future.

There is a very interesting website on physical abuse and the link is included at the end of this article as you may be amazed to know that over a million people, male and female, are abused every year in the United States. Some of these are due to alcohol consumption but it's no excuse for this kind of behavior. The figure of 1 in 5 has been used on this website to represent the number of women in the workplace that may be raped within a year. That's a frightening figure and people within the workplace who inflict this kind of harm on others need to be dealt with so that they cannot inflict that type of harm on anyone else. But do people report them? Unfortunately, because of the need for their jobs, often they do not report the action.

If you are being abused, use some of the links from the page noted at the end of this book because you need to seek help and to help deal with people who are making your work life difficult. These crimes that go unpunished need to be addressed. It doesn't just happen to women either. If you feel so afraid of going to work because of something of this nature, you do need to seek recourse through the law and be paid for your consequential losses if you should lose the employment that led to this behavior. Keep your facts straight and make sure that you have evidence of what is happening because this is the only way of stopping people like this in their tracks.

Emotional abusers

These are people within the workplace that may be promising you promotion based upon your behavior toward them. They may ask for favors. They may make you uncomfortable about what they have asked you to do and may promise to put your name in for promotion if you comply with their wishes. This kind of abuser is subtle. They hide behind the picture of respectability, but their threat can be very real. There was an Indian lady that worked in one workplace where I was a personnel officer who came to us with a complaint against someone who was threatening her. Although others may have seen this as harassment, she saw it as emotional abuse and was very upset by their behavior. In a multicultural society, the workplace is somewhere that has become a melting pot of different beliefs and if someone is behaving badly toward another member of staff and making them emotionally fear coming to work, then this behavior needs to be stemmed.

In her particular case, he was threatening to take her job away if she complained about him and was insulting her knowing that her religion did not allow her to talk in this way with males. Her husband had made a concession, letting her work because he knew it meant a lot to her, though had he known about the emotional turmoil that this man had inflicted on his wife, his recourse may not have been acceptable by western standards. They put people in prison for this kind of behavior toward women, especially respectably married ones. The personnel department investigated the case and found that indeed the man was a threat to her – that she was suffering as a result and that she could easily have sued the company and would have won had this guy been allowed to continue. He was fired and there was no question about why. The example made showed others that this kind of treatment of others was not acceptable and would not be tolerated within the office.

Companies cannot afford to have a reputation of bias against certain cultures and emotional abuse doesn't stop there. A single woman desperate to keep her job can be coerced into doing things within the workplace that she feels are unethical, based on the fact that someone is threatening her with the loss of the job if she doesn't comply. Abuse is a huge potential when you put human beings together in one place for an extended period of time and if it is happening, you need to make sure that your contract covers exactly what you are supposed to do in cases such as this. Unfortunately, those who work for people who control them in this way may not feel that they have anywhere to turn. However, they do. The Equal Employment Opportunity Commission is always interested in finding out about people who have complaints, though you need to have your complaint in writing and to be able to back it up wherever possible with statements from other employees who have been experiencing a similar thing.

Chapter 4
Bullying

To carry on from the last chapter, this chapter deals with bullying in general. A thin line separates mean behavior from bullying. Bullying is an extreme case of mean behavior in which the bully inflicts irreparable psychological and sometimes even physical damage to the victim. It can be verbal, physical or emotional. While difficult behavior can be handled well by ignoring the person, bullying can't and shouldn't be ever ignored. It can turn very ugly if not handled well in time. In worst case scenario it can also lead to suicide by the victim.

Bullying can also vary in nature and symptoms. It is very easy to confuse bullying with normal conflict. The key point in bullying is that all the actions are done repeatedly and without any reason. There might not always be a trigger. Here are few and the most common signs related to bullying:

- The culprit repeatedly picks up on a particular person or a group of people and mocks them in public.

- The culprit threatens the victim repeatedly. Threats may range from public shaming to inflicting physical harm.

- The culprit tries to entice others and spreads rumors about the victim. Most of the cases of bullying are done in groups because it is easier to demoralize the victim when he or she is completely surrounded by haters.

- The culprit tries to isolate and humiliate the victim as much as possible. He will shun the victim completely and can even neglect his or her existence.

- The culprit enjoys seeing their target in pain and discomfort. They can go any lengths to make sure that their target's life is made hell.

- A special kind of bullying called "cyber bulling" is getting common now days with the advent of the internet and advancement in technologies. Culprit can take obscene pictures of the victim or film them and threaten to release the material all over the World Wide Web. Cyber bullying is a separate arena that needs to be handled very carefully because of the involvement of professional hackers and the lack of knowledge among people. Even though the majority of population uses the internet now days, they still take online security casually. Cyber bullying is a widespread phenomenon and it can disturb the victim worse than the regular bullying because it can spread easily. In a matter of minutes, strangers from other countries might start harassing the victim and this ultimately drives the victim to take drastic measures like self-harming or committing suicide. If suffering from this, you need to be able to report the incident and log the events so that your boss can remove you from the situation. We come into contact with all kinds of people during the course of work and if someone that you contact via the Internet is harassing you, you need your boss to step in and deal with it appropriately, so that this cannot continue to happen.

How to Identify Symptoms of Bullying?

Bullying often makes the victim withdraw in a shell therefore most of the cases of bullying go unnoticed until it is too late. It is important to identify bullying as soon as possible. The delay can lead to irreversible damages to both victim and the culprit. Here is how you can notice if someone might be getting bullied:

- They'll try to avoid people as much as possible. They'll refrain from going to social gatherings, school or office. Don't confuse it with introvert nature. Some people are introvert right from the start and don't feel much comfortable surrounded by people. If you notice that the person has suddenly started acting this way from sometime back, then you might need to take matter into your hands.

- They'll start skipping office or school because of headaches or illness. They'll often fake that they are not well and try to come up with one or the other excuse to skip going to work or school. A continued absenteeism will be noticeable and it might go for a very long period.

- They'll grow quiet all of a sudden. They'll start expressing less and will often avoid or even stop sharing things with even the closest family members.

- Their nature might change drastically. Bullying can make even the most cheerful ones go into depression. You might notice less enthusiasm in their voice. They might get annoyed easily and can also become short tempered. Bullying victims are not able to fight back their abusers so they start to vent out their anger by other methods. They can get irritated easily and may show several mood swings in a day. They will become pessimist and will always talk in a gloomy tone. They will give up on their tasks and will often start skipping work deadlines. In worst cases, they might also think about running away for home.

- The best way to identify bullying is looking for signs of physical abuse. The victim might start to have a lot of injuries repeatedly and will not give proper explanation for them. If you ask about it, they'll try to dodge your question as much as possible. Victims can also harm themselves as a way to vent out their frustration. Keep an eye on the person if he or she is spending a lot of time alone and often shows wounds, cuts or bruise marks on their body.

If you believe that someone within your organization is being bullied, it's your duty, as a human being, to report it to your senior staff that can deal with it. If you have someone being bullied by senior staff, this needs taking further with the Equal Employment Opportunities Commission who will take over the investigation. It is necessary in a case like this that you provide them with full details of the breach of conduct that has led to someone becoming a victim.

Remember that victims are often afraid to discuss what has happened to them. Their abusers are very clever and will hold fear over their heads so that they do not tell others what has happened. The same goes in the schoolyard when strong people bully those who are weaker. Some carry this through to the workplace. Their behavior toward others is unacceptable. You need to be able to help people who are in this situation and if you are stronger than they are, they may need your help. If you find that someone within your workplace is exhibiting any of the signs of being abused, try to talk to them outside of the workplace where they do not feel threatened and get the truth from them so that you can help them. If they refuse to talk about it, you can't make them but you can let them know that you are there for them and that you don't want to make them worry any more than they are. Added pressure upon them may push them over the edge, so tread lightly and be kind and generous in your support.

Knowing the difference between Harassment and Bullying

Harassment in the workplace in the United States includes when someone is being singled out because of their race, religion, gender or ethnicity. If you see this happening in the workplace, it's against the law. Bullying may be more subtle, but it's every bit as harmful to those who are suffering from it. If you believe that the behavior toward a fellow member of staff is illegal, then you can talk about it with your personnel department or with a legal representative such as law enforcement officers. Be aware though that thinking about the member of staff's green card situation may be something that has to be considered as they may be deported as a result of your report. It is therefore better to deal with this within the company and try to encourage them to apply for a green card to avoid the threats that they are experiencing. Remember that you are protected against this type of treatment and the sooner you get your paperwork in order, the better because you will be able to turn it around and not allow people to use your status against you.

Psychology behind Bullying

Bullying is a very unfortunate behavior and often generates a lot of anger towards the culprit. But there are two sides to every coin. As much as it affects the victim, the culprit is also usually not a very happy person. Bullies are often a result of intense psychological trauma and this may date back to their childhood. Nobody is born a bully; it is the situation that makes them so. There might be a lot of reasons behind a person turning a bully;

one of the main reasons is domestic violence or violence within their home as they grew up.

The majority of bullies had or have a violent household. When parents ill-treat their children, the children learn this behavior and start to treat the world the same way. They develop a biased attitude towards the world and think that force is the only way to achieve power and respect. They have always seen their caretakers resorting to violence or abusive language when they didn't like something. So they acquire this trait and become very stubborn.

Some type of traumatizing incident might have also damaged the psychology of the person making bullying seem like the only option that they have to protect themselves from being hurt. Most of the bullies were themselves bullied at some point or the other in life. They developed these scars that could not heal over time and thus they feel satisfied inflicting pain on others and realizing that they are not the only ones to get bullied.

Fierce competition or jealousy might also induce the trait of bullying in some people. When people realize that they are not able to defeat their competitors, they might resort to bullying. This kind of bullying is very common in workplace and school. If children are compared excessively and unnecessarily, they might develop an unhealthy jealousy that may drive them to become bullies in later stages.

The gist of the problem is that the bullies lack a sense of comfort and love that makes them to resort to extreme measures like harming others. They are very vulnerable and weak from inside and try to mask their insecurities by proving others weak. Therefore, focus should also be given on reforming the bullies and helping them to understand their problem. If not attended, they might commit serious crimes in future and harm themselves as well as the society on a large scale.

Workplace Bullying

Workplace bullying is not a new thing, but a relatively new term in common parlance. It is difficult to identify because bullying can be confused as "work demands" and vice versa. A strong headed management can be confused with bullying when in reality it works towards providing feedbacks that are constructive for the company and the employees. In a work place, there will always be difference in opinions and your opinion might be accepted or not.

Many times for the betterment of our company, we have to take some strong actions. This shouldn't be considered as bullying. In the name of workplace bullying many false cases are being reported where the management had actually taken a right step.

Credibility of anti-bullying laws goes down with such cases and real bullying cases can go neglected. Here are the signs that fall under the category of workplace bullying

- Social Isolation and complete segregation of a colleague or employee.

- Establishing impossible deadlines that on incompletion will make the employee lose face in the department.

- Neglecting and blocking promotion, training or leave applications frequently and without any reason.

- Threatening the person to get him or her fired from his post or de promoted.

- Spreading malevolent and hateful rumors with intent to defame the victim. Framing a different meaning of the victim's statement and publicizing it with the purpose of making it reach the higher authorities.

- Trying to tamper the work of the victim. This can be done by giving wrong information about the work to the victim or physically tampering the work. Culprit can steal the documents and records of the victim or damage them so that the victim is not able to finish the given work.

- Encroaching on personal life of the victim and trying to find ways to humiliate or give stress to them.

- Changing the work guidelines frequently to confuse the victim and hamper his or her progress.

- Condemning the victim in front of everyone frequently and yelling at them or abusing them.

- Depreciating their opinions and giving them less work or taking their responsibilities away from them so that they feel "useless" in the office.

- Threatening to physically harm them or defame them, especially in the case of female employees.

Effects of Workplace Bullying

Effects of workplace bullying are not too different from the effects of bullying in other areas. But they can inflict far more damage to the victim as they disturb both the personal and the professional life of the victim. Some of them are:

- Frustration and anger that can affect relationships with other apprentices. In long run, the image of the victim gets damaged and colleagues start to maintain a distance from them.

- Loss of confidence that can drastically disturb the victim's performance in the work place.

- Psychosomatic indications like headaches and stomach pains that can increase in intensity.

- Fear and increased vulnerability to stress that can lead to frequent absenteeism from work.

- Loss of focus that can lead to decrease in productivity. The victim loses the power to concentrate on work and might remain absent minded all the time in office.

- All these symptoms lead to decrease in productivity that can ultimately hamper the progress of the company. Very good workers and professionals are lost each year to bullying since they are not able to cope up with it and ultimately quit. Companies lose people and this also shakes the customer confidence on the organization.

- Personal life of the victim can get affected drastically as they try to cope up with stress in professional front.

They might vent out their frustration on family members and this can further lead to arguments.

How to Deal with Workplace Bullying?

After learning to identify workplace bullying, it is time to learn about the ways to deal with it. This kind of bullying can damage the victim as well as disrupt the organization from inside. It is very important to identify and deal with the bully in time so that the work place environment remains healthy and comfortable for everyone.

The management team should clearly layout the guidelines for appropriate and inappropriate behavior beforehand. A separate "anti-bullying" policy should be made and its guidelines should be clearly laid down. These guidelines should be forwarded to each and every employee, from senior most position to the ground level worker. The rules should also be displayed in the work area wherever possible in the form of posters or notices. If a formal message has been given, chances are that people even with bullying streak in them would fear prosecution and therefore refrain from harassing anyone. As an employer here are the few steps you can take to avoid bullying in your organization. The policy should roughly be drafted in the following way:

- Clearly state your organization's belief against bullying and how bullying can affect lives.

- Mention the activities that will come under bullying and the ones that will not. This step is necessary to prevent bullying and also the misuse of the anti-bullying policy of the organization.

- Mention it clearly that bullies shall not be tolerated and if reported, a serious action would be taken against them. State the consequences in a clear format so that nobody takes the policy lightly.

- Motivate the employees to report any cases of bullying they observe. Encourage them to bring out the matter to administration and not fear the bully. Mention it in the policy that the identity of the complainer will remain confidential and the doubtful person shall be tracked down separately so that he or she is caught red handed.

Review the policy regularly and keep updating it according to the environment.

The best way to prevent bullying is by setting a live example. If you ever find someone yelling or borderline harassing someone, don't ignore it. Things can accelerate from a low level to high level in no time. Instead, calmly demand for a justification from the culprit then and there in front of the staff. Explain him or her properly that a different approach can always be taken while dealing with apprentices. Make them clear that if somebody has committed a mistake, there is no need to yell or shout at that person. Being strict is different from being mean.

What if your workplace doesn't have a committee specifically dedicated to deal with bullies? Or your employer is the one to harass you? Here are the ways you can come out of this situation:

- Clearly tell the person to stop and that his actions shall not be tolerated. Be firm in your approach and don't ignore the situation at any cost. If possible take help from a senior member or someone from the managing team so that your safety is ensured all the time.

- Maintain a record of every conversation between you and the bully along with the date and time of the incident. Do not delete the texts or emails in a fit of rage. This record acts as a proof against the culprit. Removing it will only loosen your case. Whenever you see the bully approaching you, prepare to record the conversation using a recorder or a hidden camera. You can also take your colleague's help by telling them to record your conversation.

- Do not retaliate no matter how much the bully entices you. Be very calm and composed and try to deal with bully without using violence or abusive words. Most of the bullies can manipulate people well, so the bully can turn any action you take against you. Although, if the bully is trying to harm you physically then don't think twice before defending yourself. Your safety comes first before any type of proceeding.

- Report the matter to a senior authority as soon as possible. Delayed action will only harm you. If the senior most authority is the one that is harassing you, do not be afraid to report the matter to an employee union or police.

Bullying is one of those problems that can get sidelined easily. It is often considered as a behavioral problem. Those around the culprit ignore it thinking that as the person will grow up, he or she will mature automatically. The victims are often told to "grow up" or stop being a "sissy".

We have to realize that bullying is a serious issue and it needs to be paid attention from a young age. If not taken care of, this problem can grow further and lead to workplace bullying. Ignorant attitude can harm the victim and the culprit both. Reforming the bully is the only solution to completely end the bullying problem.

There are rehab centers where bullies are helped and professionals solve their problems. Instead of hiding the bully in a closet, it's better to seek professional help so that their behavior can be changed as early as possible. Victims also need to be paid special attention. Those people who just suffered extreme bullying and are recovering from it should be given a lot of moral support. They should be monitored so that they don't suffer any kind of psychological damage in the future.

In the end, I would like to say that we should be always vigilant about our surroundings. If you observe any kind of bullying in your school, university or work place, don't hesitate to bring it up to the authorities. The victim might have developed a fear of the bully, but you can help them in this situation. Even if anonymously, try to report it to a senior authority as soon as possible.

Unfortunately workplace bullying is something that is current in this day and age and all you can do is prepare yourself and try to make sure that you are never placed in a situation where someone else has power over you. If you find anyone within your life crossing the line of what is acceptable to you, walk away.

Within the work place, there are ways of protecting yourself and sometimes those that threaten back off when you speak to them about it calmly and tell them that there is no way their behavior is acceptable. Tell them that you have no problem with them and that you prefer that the story ends here, without others being involved. Let them know that you know what to do if it continues.

People who are mentally weaker than others usually perform bullying and sometimes confronting it is the best way of dealing with it, letting your abuser know that you are ready to complain and even to seek legal recourse if their behavior continues.

Chapter 5
Conflict

What it really is and its sources

> *"Conflict is drama, and how people deal with conflict shows you the kind of people they are."*
>
> *-Stephen Moyer*

Now that we have already discussed what difficult behavior is, and the classically different types of person, let us now go to a serious and a very usual circumstance and event in that happens in any workplace: Conflict. Put it in simple words, it can be defined as direct opposition between ideas or interests. It arises when a person disagrees to the other person's point of views or beliefs.

William Lockhart

In any conflict situation there would always be two important factors to be considered. The objective point in which the parties do not agree on and the emotions or personal perceptions that goes along the situation. Plainly speaking, you have to be aware that in dealing with conflicts in the office you must set aside the second factor and focus on the objective facts in which the situation is supposed to be based on.

According to Blaine Donais, author of *Workplaces That Work* published by Canada Law Book, the successful administration of work environment conflict obliges a comprehension of the nature and wellsprings of conflict in the work environment. It happens when there is a view of contrary point of views between work environment members. This ought to be recognized from arguments. They are simply a by-result of conflict. They are the outward explanation of it. Run of the mill arguments come as formal court cases, grievances, contentions, dangers and counter dangers and so forth. Conflict can exist without arguments, however it doesn't exist without conflict. In any case, this conflict may not be easily noticed. Much of it exists in every working environment without transforming into arguments.

For us to deeply understand workplace conflict we first must know its sources. Though in this book we would be mostly dealing with people conflicts these could help you have a better understanding of organizational setup which includes these conflict sources that includes interpersonal, change related, external factors and organizational.

Interpersonal

Interpersonal conflict is the most apparent form of conflict in the workplace. It is not that difficult enough for you to be aware of the results of rumors, gossips and sometimes even office politics. Moreover, language and personality styles may often clash, resulting into a great deal of conflict. There are also strong racial and ethno-cultural sources of conflict as well as gender ones. These scenarios may lead to charges of harassment and judgment or at least the feeling that such things actually prevail. People also often bring their problems from home into the workplace resulting to further conflict. Another underlying reason for regarding workplace conflict can also be found in changing thoughts regarding individual achievements. The solid commute for business related accomplishment in a few members could cause conflict with members who don't underline business related achievement in their lives.

To help you reveal some sources of conflict, you may use personality testing instruments Personality Dynamics Profiles, Thomas-Kilman, FIRO-B and the very popular Myers-Briggs. Moreover there are other instruments you may use like forming of focus groups, conducting scheduled interviews and confidential surveys.

Change related (Trends)

Nowadays the workplace has increased noticeably the levels of stress and conflict due to many changes including critical downsizing and change of management. Other changes also include technological advancements and different work methodologies. Many professional are also aware of the constant reorganization that also leads to conflict. In relation to this reorganization, non-profit organizations sometimes find it necessary to shift their other work responsibilities to other related organizations. Those people who specialize in analyzing workplace behaviors of people must check the history of the organization going back as far as ten years to know the level of churn that has already occurred. Generally, the greater and recent the change is, the more significant the conflict will be expected.

External Factors

These factors could be sum up to evolving markets, effects of approving free trade amongst countries, foreign and domestic competition, and recession that also results to economic pressures. Conflict emerges with customers and suppliers effecting client administration and conveyance of products.

Additionally, non-profit organizations specifically could face political pressures and demands form particular vested parties. Government change may have a great impact on every organization may it be public or not. Those organizations dependent on government funding could change their funding levels dramatically. Public philosophies could also have an effect on the system of treating employees and also on the way those who are in the higher management view them upon.

To search for outer elements of conflict, have an audit of the connections between the subject association and different associations. Organizations or government offices that have steady associations with outsiders will discover this to be a significant source of conflict for workplace members.

Organizational

There are various sources of conflict on this one. Those identifying with hierarchy and the lack of ability to resolve contradicting interests are very prevalent in many work environments. Due to power differences labor and employee tensions are heightened. The differences in management and leadership styles between departments can also be a source of conflict. It could also include seniority, pay balance and work style conflict. This type of dissonance may arise over the dissemination of responsibilities, resource allocation, types of work and benefits, distinctive levels of resistance for risk taking, and changing perspectives on responsibility. What's more, conflict can emerge where there are seen or genuine contrasts in treatment between divisions or gatherings of representatives.

A careful survey of the work environment is recommended for such sources of conflict. Again reviews, meetings and focus groups can help uncover these sources. Furthermore, organizational sources can be anticipated based upon best practices from comparable associations. All associations experience such conflict. Much can be found out from the lessons of comparative associations who have made an investigation of these sources of conflict.

Chapter 6
Cooling Conflicts

Foolproof methods on how to keep your cool dealing with difficult people

Steps on how to deal with Conflicts

1. Learn how to control your temper and manage the conflict face to face. It may seem to be a primitive process to solve any kind of conflicts nowadays without the use of technologies, specifically through communication gadgets. But it is proven that meeting an individual face to face is frequently the most ideal approach to go. Up close and personal correspondence is more successful than different structures in light of the fact that it takes into consideration a dynamic trade of data. It gives you the chance to make utilization of the handshake, a grin, eye contact, hand motions and other critical non-verbal

communication. It likewise permits you to watch vital nonverbal signs from the other party. Put aside time to meet with the individual up close and personal at a commonly advantageous time and spot. At the point when conceivable, meet on "unbiased turf" as opposed to one of your workplaces so nobody has the "home court" advantage.

2. Show you get it. Utilize the expression 'I see'. However utilize it with enough careful consideration. You can show yourself as being supportive or somehow knowing by simply saying that you do understand. It additionally welcomes the reaction, 'What do you signify, "you get it"? How might you be able to possibly know such thing?' It is nothing but better to always try to maximize the power of understanding and wide thinking but you may use it a practically different way. You may try saying "You know my friend, some time ago I've experienced the same thing when I got into a real argument with someone from my past. I was very furious and upset that time and I can feel that you are feeling that same thing I felt right now. Honestly speaking, I really do understand what you have been going through." Making things a little bit more personal makes the situation less bad and a lot easier to handle. Always remember that you should be the one with

a wider understanding a higher level of patience. Try not to scoop down into the level of the other person who you are dealing with. Stick to the idea that the other person has issues that you are not experiencing and so better to understand more.

3. Show gratitude and learn how to ask first. The capacity to convey what needs be unmistakably will permit you to say what's at the forefront of your thoughts, request what you need and require and express what is on your mind. There is an expression that an issue all around expressed is an issue half-fathomed. Through this you can prevent further damage that may lead to a conflict. Why make a solicitation? Step one, reasoning of the right demand to make gives a nanosecond to you to put the matches away and disregard lighting the wire. Second, it stops you transforming an issue into a more extensive clash.

4. Who says it is not easy to walk away from certain clashes or conflict? Of course if caught into an unfriendly situation you may not want to continue to stay as an easy target to annoy or be tripped upon by those rude and arrogant or somehow insensitive people. It is human nature to avoid all chaos that could occur to them. Every people, including those who are in the workplace have the right to flee away

from these people if they already feel threatened or uncomfortable.

5. Mock the person you are dealing with in a proper manner. In an instance you may just have to repeat what he have said to you in an ethical way like, "You're aware that you've been saying this kind of stuffs to me...." The chances are, the point at which the individual has heard what he or she has said, he or she will perceive how improper on the other hand terrible it is and cool off. Once in a while you need to rehash the words more than once. This strategy keeps the emphasis on one issue and keeps the discussion from diverting itself from an irredeemable tallness.

6. Admit and explain how you truly feel in a proper manner. Say to the person you have conflict with the reason for being furious or angry by letting him know what he did that made you upset. Explain properly what you truly feel yet preventing to sound like you put the blame on him.

7. Acknowledge your mistakes. In a proper manner one must know how to deal with the conflict he had started. Be mindful you could call your own part in making the contention. In the event that you've done something incorrectly or unseemly, be willing to recognize it and say you're sad, regardless of the fact that the contention is not

by any stretch of the imagination an after effect of your activities. Now and then you need to meet individuals most of the way to get to where you need to go.

8. Control your emotions. Get a tight grasp on poise and clutch your coolness. The more you work on being quiet, the better you will get at it. At the point when clash gazes you in the face, say to yourself, this is an open door for me to act naturally controlled, quiet and loose. While it may appear glaringly evident, pausing a minute to yourself before you respond is a standout amongst the best approaches to hold that temper under control.

9. Manage to have a conciliator. On the off chance that a circumstance is especially unstable or troublesome and different endeavors have not lived up to expectations, you may welcome a nonpartisan outsider, for example, a boss, to go about as a go between if this is pleasing to all concerned. A go between can stay target, listen to both sides, and encourage determination and trade off. Be firm on your goals; you're there to determine a contention, not vanquish an adversary.

10. Analyze first the situation before dealing with it. Before tending to the individual with whom you have a contention, consider talking about the circumstance with

a target companion or relative. This can help to clear up issues and needs. Look for criticism and exhortation in managing the circumstance. Be that as it may, be mindful so as not to depend on the assessment of an included outsider who may have his or her own particular motivation. Arranging your procedure, including what you need to say, and afterward record it and practice it. Make a note card, if important, with your principle ideas. This will help you to feel all the more in control and keep focused.

11. Put an effort to resolve the conflict. You must work on it. Make moves to minimize clash at work before it happens. Work at growing great associations with collaborators and partners. Become more acquainted with individuals. Be neighborly and agreeable. Everybody has diverse needs and needs and originates from distinctive social foundations. As opposed to what you've heard, commonality breeds regard.

12. Avoid negative people and the troublemakers for they will always put you down and out your temper in to your limits. Learn how to deal with them and better to ignore them. They will suck you in and drag you down. Try not to take part in tattle or manipulating. Get the realities before

forming a hasty opinion about something you're heard through the grapevine. Know when it's fitting to leave a showdown, and constantly consider the source notwithstanding feedback or frightful remarks.

13. Do not try to avoid your conflict if necessary. On the off chance that you disregard or maintain a strategic distance from it, it can prompt expanded anxiety and uncertain sentiments of displeasure, threatening vibe and disdain. When you figure out how to oversee clash adequately, you'll be more satisfied and healthier, physically and inwardly. You'll have better connections. You'll be a superior pioneer, a superior colleague and a superior individual. You'll pick up appreciation, enhance your self-regard and manufacture fearlessness. You'll get a greater amount of what you need.

Your part in any given situation at work

We said right at the beginning of this book that you play a part in the relationships that you create at work. Your part in this relationship can anger others. You are not immune from being a difficult person. It's important to examine each relationship that you have in the workplace and decide if you are contributing to the problem in any way. You may be and you may not be aware of it. The thing is that when you gather so many people together in one place, not everyone can get on. There will be characters that you don't particularly like and there will be people you may be a little jealous of or who perhaps do not have the same temperament as you. That's a very important thing to consider.

Teams

If you are part of a team and find any particular member of that team really makes you angry or upset, you may need to look at your own attitude toward them as other people may not find their behavior unreasonable. Let's try and examine the kinds of reasons why you may be having difficulty with someone in a team situation:

- They belittle you
- You find them difficult
- They waste time
- They don't let you put your ideas forward

Unfortunately, there's actually no real rule against people who make you feel less valuable, so to a certain degree, you have to see if it's you that is being too sensitive or whether your complaints are valid. For example, is the person known for belittling people or do they just pick on you? Have you talked about it with others? Perhaps others felt like this as well until they got accustomed to working with this person. You need to find out if it's personal or whether it's their attitude in general that annoys you. The thing is that what can be done about it may be limited unless you can actually prove that it's vindictive and aimed specifically toward you.

A better way forward is to think of the psychological approach that you have to your work. For example, if you know that someone is predictably rude to you, they will also be accustomed to your response. Perhaps they get pleasure out of seeing you squirm. Stop squirming. You may find that they gain more respect for you and stop singling you out. You do need to examine the way that you handle relationships because sometimes strong people pick on the weaker members of the team because they can. Take away that ability by letting their comments slide, and you may be able to relax more and enjoy your work more.

If you find someone is difficult, from what aspect do you find them difficult? You have to define what it is that makes you see them as difficult. Perhaps they see you in the same way. Often we form views of people too early and in the workplace, this kind of bias can work against us. Look closely at the relationship and find out what it is that annoys you. I could write a list of things that annoy me about one of my current colleagues but none of them were really valid enough reasons for me to take any action other than that outlined below and that was socially:

- He dresses too loudly
- He always has to make his voice heard
- He isn't tolerant of others

These are all personal points of view. The way that someone dresses is really dictated by the dress code of the company and is none of my concern. Yes, it irks me, but it's really nothing that should stop me from doing my job. I find it amusing in some ways, and it's his other habits that get my back up. For example, I have never understood people who have to make their voices heard over the top of everyone else's. It's almost as if they need to validate their being there. Looking into this, I found that people who act in this way generally do so because they lack confidence. I talked further with this employee and found out quite a lot about his family. His brothers were successful and he had always played second fiddle to them. The workplace was his only outlet. In his marriage, for example, the family always put him down because he wasn't as successful as his brothers. His house was smaller, his income was smaller and his wife didn't come from a rich family like his brother's wives.

For a long time I tried to work out my part in the situation. If something was annoying me that much, there had to be a reason. I took the guy to lunch. He was actually very good at doing his job and when I explained that he didn't need to compensate for stuff and didn't need to shout quite so much, he laughed. He was amused because he hadn't really thought of it before in that way. By being kind, I was able to ascertain that he thought he had to fight for validation within the office because of the way his family treated him. When he quietened down and started to dress a little more normally, things improved.

His tolerance of others was something he had to work on, but I could see where it was coming from. Every time he had a criticism, he made it larger than it was because he was so accustomed to being put down by his family. I joked with him to lighten up – it wasn't the end of the world and gradually he accepted that in fact he didn't need to fight so hard. When he was himself and didn't try so hard to be something that was not who he was, we actually liked him.

People who waste time

These are the freeloaders in life and every workplace has one or two. Again, you can't do much about it but let them know that you know they are not pulling their weight. If they are true freeloaders, they are pretty thick skinned and will continue to try and get by getting a salary they don't actually deserve. The thing that you need to think when freeloaders upset you is that everyone has to live with their own Karma. If they put nothing in, they can't expect to get much back.

I have a saying that helps me to cope with this kind of person. "What goes around comes around" and what that implies is that we get out of life what we merit. If he wants to be a freeloader, he won't get much because the price of being accepted and being a really valuable worker is hard work. If you do nothing, you don't gain friends. You don't gain promotion. You are yourself stuck because relationships are a little like that. You get out of a relationship what you put into it and if you don't, there is some kind of imbalance that needs to be addressed.

Of all the types of people that you will work with over the course of a lifetime, take comfort from the fact that some people will leave a lasting impression for all the right purposes. These will be the mentors, the people who you respect and the people who left some kind of mark that you can't put aside easily. These may be few and far between but they really do make up for the people who make your working life difficult and actually give you the impetus to try and succeed regardless of the idiots you have to put up with in your day to day life.

The Qualities that Make a Person Likeable

You need to see both sides of the coin and should first look into your own approach and then look at the approach of your colleagues. Somewhere along the line, if you are unhappy in your work, there will be an imbalance that needs to be addressed either by you or by them. Don't expect that all of the bad things are the responsibility of someone else. If you look at the way that mindfulness works, it works in a very clever way. When you observe things around you, you simply observe. You don't judge. When you can adopt this attitude, it not only makes work situations a lot easier to bear, it makes you more bearable.

The qualities that I am going to outline in this chapter are qualities that you should be displaying toward people that you work with and which you should expect from them in exchange. If you can look back on your experience at work and compare this list of qualities with the experiences you have had with people during your working career, you will see that there may have been times when you were difficult for others to work with and times when others may have found you equally difficult. Working with difficult people and being able to handle them includes adjusting the way that you see others, because that's where the big secret lies.

Supposing you have a work colleague who is on a diet. You keep offering her biscuits because you have a generous nature and she gets fatter and loses no weight. She could blame you for being thoughtless bearing in mind her circumstances. It isn't very kind giving someone on a diet all these calories. She could blame you for her failure. However, in reality – she owns her own life and all that she needed to do in those circumstances was say "no." You can see from these circumstances that there were two people involved in a situation and that each had their own individual approach. It was the way that the approach was perceived that was important. You have more power than you give yourself credit for. If someone wants to make you angry, it only works if you permit it to happen. So how do you stop this from happening? You observe, you do not judge. When you learn to do that, you have cracked it!

Honesty

No one likes being lied to. Thus, honesty is one of the first principles that you need to adhere to. If you are asked your ideas about a job or are asked what your opinion is, be honest, even if you feel that your opinion may not be popular with others. Be honest in your dealings with others and expect them to be equally honest.

Integrity

Are you trustworthy? When people ask you things can they trust your answers? Integrity comes from proving yourself to be of value. If someone questions your integrity, you should ask yourself how trustworthy you were in those given circumstances. Sometimes, we pass the buck. Sometimes we blame others for our own shortcomings. Before people in the workplace can trust your integrity, you have to demonstrate that it's worth trusting.

Are you friendly and encouraging?

This is vital to getting on with other people, but sometimes people overdo it. They try to compensate for their lack of social skills by being too up close and personal too quickly. Have you ever met someone who insisted they call you by your first name before you even know them? Sometimes people like this make you feel terribly uncomfortable. Be careful when you make new relationships in the workplace. Keep a polite distance and let yourself get to know them gradually without being cold. Relationships are a real balancing act sometimes and people may appear more difficult than they actually are because you may have taken their friendship for granted too early. The best way out of this situation is to back off a little bit and maybe apologize for your over-zealousness but tell the person who you made uncomfortable that you meant nothing by it and it was your nervousness at the new job that perhaps made you over keen to fit in.

Patience

Patience is one of the most valuable attributes that you can have in the workplace. If you are having problems with someone else, were you patient enough? Not everyone learns at the same rate and sometimes that patience will make the difference between whether you are accepted by people or not. Sometimes when you are training people, you can come over as being a little intimidating if you don't have the level of patience that it requires and that's important. Before blaming others for being unresponsive to your training, ask yourself if you were patient enough and if those learning from you were able to achieve what you set out for them to achieve. If not, you may have to adjust your teaching methods to help them to grasp the concept that you are trying to pass on. Sometimes, simply exercising patience and realizing that everyone needs a certain amount of time to adjust to new things can overcome that difficulty.

Impatience tends to show itself off in different ways. Are you short with people who don't learn at the rate you want them to? In fact, students who take vacation jobs often look down on their fellow workers but they forget these people have chosen that job as a career, while the student may only be in that environment temporarily. Thus, the student without patience may actually upset fellow staff by looking down on them. It's worthwhile remembering that there is a need in the world for all levels of intelligence and you should never deride fellow workers just because you feel that your education is better than theirs.

Willing

Sometimes people are unwilling to do things that they feel are demeaning. For example, a secretary may feel it is beneath her to make cups of coffee in the office, but in this case, perhaps she needs to get over her own superiority and just join in. You make better relationships in a company when you are willing to become part of the team instead of holding yourself apart from the team. Animosity can be caused inadvertently by trying to be superior. If you are one of those people who have done this, maybe making a cup of coffee for everyone will change their attitude toward you. In the workplace, there's no such task as one that is beneath you. Remember that, and you will find that you are more open to meeting people from all different levels and meeting them on equal terms. That's vital to relationships. Imagine if you did that to a friend. The friend would soon feel that you were unwilling to do something you felt was beneath you and you would certainly lose that give and take that relationships are all about.

Your willingness to give should be equal to others' willingness and never because of your feeling of superiority. This really will cause waves because if you put yourself over as superior or above the task at hand you are, at the same time, implying that those who perform that task are lower on the ladder than you are. That's not actually accurate. All employees are equal no matter how lowly their duties.

Exercises to Help Your Patience Levels

Although any conflict that you are experiencing may not be due to your interaction with someone else, it helps if you know how to deal with difficult people in the best way possible and make this a habit in your life. There are several roads that you can take which will help you to deal with difficult people. You may want to ask at work if there is a course available in Neuro Linguistic programming because this is very useful from a managerial standpoint and opens up a much more successful kind of dialog with people because it looks into the different elements that go into communication. If you have a greater understanding of these, this helps you to be able to see things from a different perspective and thus be more efficient in your communication skills.

If you don't want to go that far, one skill that may help you is mindfulness or indeed taking up meditation because it slows the

Difficult People

thinking processes down sufficiently to stop you from reacting without hindsight and that's where a lot of problems start. Mindfulness incorporates observing without judgment and that's pretty hard to learn but when you can do that, you get a greater understanding of people and you don't react too quickly. You also learn to put aside your personal prejudices and see the bigger picture that is always useful when dealing with people who are problematic. For example, look at the scenario below and you can see where the lack of communication didn't help the situation.

Employee A and very annoyed by Employee B. Employee A sees that employee B is taking credit all of the time for other people's work. Employee A is angry about it and his first reaction would be to voice that anger. However, this doesn't help things because what happens when you voice anger is that it upsets everyone within the workplace. When you look at the situation using mindfulness, Employee A would examine what was happening more deeply. He would look at the cases where Employee B was taking the credit for another person's work and would analyze the situation a little better. There would be no anger, but there would be solutions to ensure that the employee was not able to continue this bad practice. No one gets annoyed. There is no action that upsets everyone. Instead, there is a thought process going on that comes to a logical conclusion that suits everyone.

Practicing Mindfulness

To get used to mindfulness, try it at home. Observe things that are happening in your family life. Observe the world around you. Be aware of tastes, sensations and everything that is happening in the moment. That's the hardest thing for people to do because they are too filled with prejudices from the past or worry about the future. Think that this moment is all that you have and thus that you need to make the most of it. When you eat food, don't swallow it down too quickly. Instead, taste the flavors, feel the textures. It takes quite a while to think in the moment. We are too accustomed to being elsewhere in our thoughts but when you are dealing with any kind of problem in your life, and that includes dealing with difficult people within the workplace, your calming influence really will help you in your dealings and make life a lot easier for you to bear.

One of the things that human beings are particularly good at is being petty. When you see things in perspective, you tend not to internalize so much and build up anger and resentment. You also know how to deal with situations that arise because you are able to put all of your concentration into that moment, instead of facing it with negative feelings such as anger, jealousy or any other negative attitude.

Breathing is also a part of mindfulness that will help you to deal with difficult people because when situations and people worry you, you tend to over-oxygenate. If you know how to control your breathing, that won't happen and you won't get as hot under the collar. This means that you can deal with your day to day dealings in a much cooler manner.

To breathe correctly, you need to breathe in through the nose, hold the breath for a moment and then breathe out through the nose. There should be a pivoting action in your upper abdomen and that's important. It helps you to inhale and exhale in a much more regular fashion and if you are conscious of your breathing, that also means that you are unlikely to suffer from a rise in blood pressure or over oxygenating when someone is difficult with you. This makes you stronger and more capable of dealing with bad situations calmly.

You may think that this has nothing to do with difficult people but it has everything to do with them. Your reaction to anything is to do with YOU. Let me try and demonstrate this further, showing you what a difference it makes to the way that you respond to difficult people.

Your boss loads the work onto you and you know that there is too much for you to handle. He doesn't do this to others. For some reason, he treats you differently to the others and seems to have a grudge against you. You can see the work piling up and you are worried about finishing it. How would you deal with this?

- Complain about it?
- Say nothing and get worried inside?
- Work out a system whereby you can manage to do it?

The person who uses mindfulness would fully assess the situation. They would work out priorities and would then tackle things in the best way possible, putting high priority jobs through first and then going on to do less important ones. They may also explain to the boss that they will try their best but that the load they have been given is a little heavy. They may even ask the boss which work should be given priority, thus leaving the boss to make that decision. They may also approach the whole situation with a sense of humor – knowing that negativity added into the mix will make it worse.

You see, the moment you respond with negativity and emotions, that's the moment you give in to the situation. You allow it to enter your head as a problem and you also allow it to hurt you. You have to see the workplace for what it is. It is a place where a certain amount of work gets done for a certain amount of hours each week. If you are expected to do more than that, square it with the boss so that you do the priority work and he has no reason to complain at the end of the day when you go home.

I have seen many workers reduced to tears over being overloaded. If you see someone in the workplace in this situation, help them out. They may just be the ally that you need to help you when you are overloaded. Situations such as this are common, as are arguments and disagreements. Don't let negativity into your life. When a situation occurs where someone is expecting you to react in a negative way, be positive. Remember that negativity is wasted on people that don't care. They have achieved what they wanted to achieve if you end up in tears. Instead of doing that, smile and be pleasant and don't show that you have hassled by it or phased by whatever it is that they have said. You have this moment. This moment is important and negativity wastes it.

Similarly, if someone is trying to show you up as incompetent, your tears confirm that you are incompetent. What they prove is that you are unable to deal with that amount of stress. It doesn't help your case to get angry and upset. It worsens it. You can then be accused of being too emotional and your tears would confirm that.

Mindfulness really does work. It stops you from reacting in a negative way. You see the work piling up and accept that it's just the way it is. You sort your work into priorities and make sure that you meet the urgent priorities. I used to do this on a regular basis and when you stop worrying about it, you actually achieve more than you thought possible and may eventually reach the bottom of the basket. People who treat you badly in the workplace do so for reactions. If they get none, then they see their effort as pointless and will usually desist.

Above all else, remember that you need to treat people as you expect to be treated. That's vital to getting on with others in a forced situation such as a workplace. In a social situation, it's much different. You choose to be with the people that you mix with. However, in a workplace situation, you don't. It's as simple as that.

We have tried to outline the different types of people and the coping mechanisms that will help you to deal with all kinds of situations. This chapter was to introduce you to alternative methods and these work very well with people who don't expect to be greeted with a smile. They expect reactions and when they don't get it, usually turn to find someone else they can get reactions from.

Why People are Difficult in General

You may be wondering why people have to be so difficult. The fact is that we all are in our own ways. If you look at people within your life, it's certain that they all do things that annoy you, or at least that most of them do. Kids at home may have their music turned on too high. Your partner may not put the trash out or your mother-in-law may try to exert power under your roof sometimes and they all have valid reasons why they do these things. They are all trying to be individuals.

When children turn on the loud music, they are trying to discover who they are and make a mark on others that they are individual and have their own choices of what they like and dislike. In the same way, people in the workplace have different backgrounds, cultures, belief systems and also different levels of intellect. You can't expect harmony when you put so many different types of people together. It's not practical. The people that annoy you are probably not doing it intentionally.

The girl in the office who can't make her mind up about which job to do first isn't trying to be awkward. She is a person who is unsure of herself, has little confidence, wants to impress and needs someone else to make the decision for her – at least until she has gained a little more confidence. Ask her "Which job do you think is the most important?" and she may waver in her answers. You can't take away responsibility from people like this because it makes their indecisiveness worse. They already have a lack of confidence. You can teach them to make the right decisions. "Mrs. Willis needs this by 4 and Mr. Ellis doesn't need this until 6" doesn't tell her exactly what she should do, but it helps her understand priorities a little better and if you help her to gain confidence, the problem can be solved on its own over the course of time when she is comfortable in her work.

The man with the loud voice is probably compensating for something too. Perhaps within his own home, he never gets a voice. Perhaps he feels it is the only way of getting heard. Sit down with him. Talk to him and if he starts talking too loudly, tell him so. It's not a big deal at all and you can do it without even being rude. "I'm sorry John, I have an ear problem. Can you keep the pitch down a bit please?" In this way, you blame yourself and he will be more than willing to comply. If you have someone whose voice is disrupting others, that person needs to be told or you need to shift the office around so that his voice doesn't disrupt others.

There is usually a very logical way to deal with people. Troublemakers or those who want to spread gossip within the office are the worst types. These are people who thrive on drama and the creation of drama. You should know from working with them that they will blow things out of all proportion and spread gossip to amuse themselves. There was once an employee like this in our workplace and we decided that spreading a rumor could backfire on her.

A very serious girl in the office was talking about a news story that she had heard on the morning TV about a pepper shortage. She said that the story had told her that supermarkets were bracing themselves for the rush because there was a world shortage. Our troublemaker took this to heart and spread the rumor all over the office and we were highly amused at the end of the day to find that 24 people had been out at lunchtime and stocked up with dozens of pots of pepper. When the joke was announced, she felt extremely foolish but it stopped her from spreading rumors or at least from people listening to them.

You have to be creative sometimes and find solutions for the problems that occur within the office that hurt no one. If you add to the hurt, you are every bit as bad as them. If you can come up with solutions that hurt no one but that help the office to become a place people actually look forward to being, this is really positive. Teamwork is also imperative under some circumstances. If you have teams working in your workplace and there seems to be some upset – you can start to have events that encourage teamwork such as quiz nights as these really do solidify friendships and get people working together. Sports do the same thing sometimes as well.

William Lockhart

Difficult people will always exist. By avoiding becoming one of them, you allow yourself the benefit of making friendships. The only exception to this is when there is some form of abuse. In the case of psychological or physical abuse, the best way out of the situation is to distance yourself from it and report it if at all possible so that the same abuse does not happen to another employee because you were too afraid to say anything.

Conclusion

If after all the while reading this book with so much discussion about troublesome, difficult and pain in the neck individuals is discouraging you, think of those persons who make you feel happy, the people who delight you, the ones who you anticipate seeing and who lighten up your life, throwing away certain negative vibes. Try to focus more on them and those partners who are a joy to work with and the partners who are dependable, legitimate and transparent.

In the chapters that have been presented to you are years of experience and at a managerial and non-managerial level. Thus you should be able to glean from them that there are ways that you can handle difficult people without becoming fretful and feeling threatened by them. The more reaction that you give to those who seek reaction, the more likely you are to be picked on. These people are looking for reaction. If you don't give them what they seek, you are not validating their actions and they will look elsewhere. Unfortunately, the world is filled with people such as this and it's a fact of life that they are so sad within their lives that they feel the need to make others equally as unhappy as they are. When you learn to let their words go over your head and don't react, they soon tire of their games.

People who play mind games are a little more dangerous, though again, are looking for reactions. When you think of abusive marriages, you may wonder why people stay in them. The fact is that there are different types of people. There are weak and strong people and those who end up becoming abusers are usually the strong who seek out the weak because they know that this gives them power that they don't otherwise have in their lives. The weak, on the other hand, lose what little power they have and feel overwhelmed by the abuse and become afraid to leave.

It is basic but people nowadays seem to have forgotten the benefits it may give and how could it help our daily lives. It is being overshadowed by email, text messaging and information transmission. The basic and best apparatuses are likely around your work area, at this time. They are pen and paper. Do not underestimate the powers of handwritten messages. A simple but sincere personal made thank you card, a letter made to acknowledge certain job well done can do have a big and changing impact on those persons around you.

Wrapping everything up in this book, I want to instill to you that handling difficult people is not truly hard if you personally know how to handle yourself first. Know your strengths, focus on them and utilize them in dealing with a difficult person. As for your weaknesses, try to learn what they are so that you can develop your own personality and improve who you are and how people see you. As nobody is perfect you can only do so much to handle others and it's vital that you first learn to handle who you are. I have added in the part about mindfulness because in today's workplace this is even more relevant than it has ever been. Those who are mindful and who employ neuro linguistic programming techniques will reach management because they are also learning about dealing with others in the most effective way and that's what management material needs to learn.

Look for programs that help you to develop a thick skin, but still be sensitive enough to feel empathy. There's a real line to be drawn when it comes to boundaries in the workplace and knowing where acceptable boundaries lie, but when you establish this balance, you usually find that respect comes with it and that people become less difficult to deal with. The most important thing that you can take to the workplace is honesty, integrity and the ability to deal with all kinds of people and make them feel equally important in the chain of command. Learn to trust people more and learn which people are the most trustworthy. Learn to delegate correctly and to help others within the workplace to become better employees. Sometimes those that are not heard get upset because the trust is lacking and this gets interpreted in different ways by different employees.

If, at the end of the day, you have to deal with difficult people, ask yourself these three questions before you actually try to come up with conclusions:

- How much of this attitude am I responsible for?

- What was lacking in the training of this employee that could have made the situation better?

- How can we move forward and address the employee's concern?

That's what personnel officers deal with every day within the workplace and it's really as simple as that. Once you work out the answers to these questions, you have all the answers that you need to deal with that difficult person. Let's look at these answers:

- I should have known better than to place these two employees together

- I need to make sure that the training of the person is done by someone more sympathetic

- I can split up the employees with the conflict and place someone else there

In this case scenario, you took responsibility in part for the situation and found a solution that suited everyone. While not all situations will be that clear cut, the first place to look for answers is within yourself. The rest follows as a matter of logic and you may find the difficult employees can be trained to become less difficult once you have a clear understanding of their grievances, personality conflicts and worries.

I want to thank you once again for choosing this book and I hope you found it informative.

Links of interest to readers:

Sexual abuse in the workplace:

http://www.workplacesrespond.org/learn/the-facts/the-costs-of-sexual-violence

William Lockhart

LÄBORG Rep: 502.592.52
Ribba Frame white 000.780.32
Blade 000.780.51

Rosaleen 120571
120571
0117

Ri

17278961R00096

Printed in Great Britain
by Amazon